WORDS THAT HURT
WORDS THAT HEAL

11/04

Dear Avi

So sorry I was out of town + had to miss your Big day. You were a treat to have in class last year. I hope you are continuing in tichon this year. Keep your spirit + leadership q you will go far. Always trust yourself

Mazel Tov

Warmly
Sally
Stodden

By Rabbi Joseph Telushkin

NONFICTION

Nine Questions People Ask About Judaism
(with Dennis Prager)
Why the Jews? The Reason for Anti-Semitism
(with Dennis Prager)
*Jewish Literacy: The Most Important Things to Know About the Jewish
Religion, Its People, and Its History*
Jewish Humor: What the Best Jewish Jokes Say About the Jews
*Jewish Wisdom: Ethical, Spiritual, and Historical Lessons from the Great
Works and Thinkers*

FICTION

The Unorthodox Murder of Rabbi Wahl
The Final Analysis of Dr. Stark
An Eye for an Eye

WORDS THAT HURT

WORDS THAT HEAL

How to Choose Words
Wisely and Well

RABBI JOSEPH TELUSHKIN

QUILL
WILLIAM MORROW
New York

Library of Congress Cataloging-in-Publication Data

Telushkin, Joseph, 1948–
    Words that hurt, words that heal / Joseph Telushkin.
        p.   cm.
    Includes bibliographical references and index.
    ISBN 0-688-16350-5
    1. Oral communication—Moral and ethical aspects.   2. Ethics
Jewish.   I. Title.
P95.T35   1995
296.3'85672—dc20   95-1116
                                                                        CIP

Printed in the United States of America

First Quill Edition 1998

14 16 18 20 19 17 15 13

BOOK DESIGN BY KATY RIEGEL

www.williammorrow.com

For Shlomo Telushkin,
of blessed memory, and
Bernard "Bernie" Resnick,
of blessed memory

My father and my uncle:
two men of golden tongues and golden hearts,
whose words healed all who knew them

Acknowledgments

A number of friends, colleagues, and family members generously gave of their time to read drafts of this book. They provided me with critical feedback, suggestions for additional material, and, equally important, the kind of enthusiastic response that motivated me to keep working on improving it. I would like to thank Dr. Stephen Marmer, Professor David Ellenson, Dr. Antonio Wood, Rabbi Leonid Feldman, Rabbi David Woznica, Rabbi Michael Paley, Helen Telushkin, Shalva Siegel, Dr. Howard Siegel, Jeff Davidowitz, Esther Davidowitz, Cori Drasin, Kirk Douglas, and Jeff Sagansky. I am grateful as well to Lauren Janis, whose rush weekend typing efforts helped me to finally finish the manuscript, and to my friend Jonathan Mark, associate editor of *The Jewish Week,* who provided me with background information on one of the cases discussed in this book.

Chapter 12, "Words That Heal," was deeply influenced by the writings of, and books edited by, Rabbi Jack Riemer, a distinguished colleague who has done pathbreaking work in this area. It was he as well who first brought to my attention the extraordinary article by Art Buchwald on the ability of kind words to heal the world.

My wife, Dvorah, helped me refine many of my ideas during hours of discussion. She also stepped in at a point when I couldn't finish an important chapter and, with seeming effortlessness, suggested exactly what I needed to do. She was entirely correct, and it was her suggestion that enabled me, after two weeks of increasingly mounting frustration, to finish the book.

If by any chance I have inadvertently omitted someone's name, I deeply apologize.

This is the fourth book on which I have worked with David Szonyi. As always, his editorial and stylistic emendations improved my writing immensely. As I have often remarked, David is a blessing to any writer.

I am deeply grateful to Uriella Obst, whose editorial and stylistic suggestions, and the fresh perspective that she brought to the manuscript, aided me greatly in improving this book.

At William Morrow and Company, I have been blessed with two wonderful editors, Ann Bramson and Gail Kinn. Their extraordinary abilities, enthusiasm, and critical intelligence are a joyous gift to any writer. When they felt something was not working, they told me exactly what was needed, and despite my initial trepidations over some of their critiques, I usually found them to be on target. In addition, their passionate excitement about the book's message has been a continuing source of inspiration to me. I am also grateful to Elisa Petrini, who acquired the book for Morrow, and whose discussions with me of the book's ideas did so much to shape its structure. My deep thanks as well to Sonia Greenbaum, a superb copy editor.

This is the ninth book on which Richard Pine has represented me. It is difficult to find a fresh way of thanking such an extraordinary person, extraordinary friend, and extraordinary agent.

I am extremely indebted to Senators Connie Mack of Florida and Joseph Lieberman of Connecticut, and their aides Ellen Bork and Nina Bang-Jensen, for their work in sponsoring legislation to establish a nationally observed "Speak No Evil Day," on May 14 (the text of the senators' legislation is found in the Appendix). I was touched by their receptivity to the idea when I first met with them, and by their continual efforts to establish this day. I am deeply grateful to my friends Max and Suzanne Singer for their help.

I would also like to acknowledge my dear friends Jean and the late Dr. Bernard Kaplan of blessed memory, of Alexandria, Louisiana, two remarkable models of ethical speech and of so much else.

My father, Shlomo Telushkin, and my uncle Bernie Resnick, both of blessed memory, were two of the kindest, noblest, human beings I have known. My father combined within himself two traits that usually do not comfortably coexist—passionate convictions and nonjudgment toward others. He had the ability to make very different kinds of people feel totally accepted, which was a large part of his wonderful graciousness. Even during the last eighteen months of his life, when he was largely paralyzed from a stroke and often in terrible pain, he never failed to thank anyone who did the slightest favor for him. Dvorah, who met him only when he was already ill, still marvels at how appreciated and loved he made her feel.

My uncle Bernie also was a first-rate mensch. When my

grandfather, Rabbi Nissen Telushkin of blessed memory, asked him as a favor to meet with a poor woman who had a legal problem—Bernie was a lawyer—he took the woman into his office right away, ahead of two clients who were waiting in his office. The woman told my grandfather with astonishment what Bernie had done. Bernie explained to my grandfather that the paying clients "would assume that a very important case had come up, which is why I was seeing this woman on such short notice, and, as a result, they wouldn't feel insulted. But, if I had made this woman wait until I had dealt with all my other clients, she would have felt that I saw her as a charity case, and would have felt humiliated."

I miss them both deeply, and feel privileged to be able to dedicate this book in their honor.

Contents

Contents

Who is the person who is eager for life,
who desires years of good fortune?
Guard your tongue from speaking evil,
and your lips from deceitful speech.

—Psalms 34:13–14

Introduction

Over the past decade, whenever I have lectured throughout the country on "Words That Hurt, Words That Heal: How to Choose Words Wisely and Well," I've asked my listeners if they can go for twenty-four hours without saying any unkind words about, or to, anybody.

Invariably, a minority raise their hands signifying yes, some people laugh, while quite a large number call out, "No!"

"All of you who can't answer yes," I respond, "must recognize how serious a problem you have. Because if I asked you to go for twenty-four hours without drinking liquor, and you said, 'I can't do that,' I'd tell you, 'Then you must recognize that you're an alcoholic.' And if I asked you to go for twenty-four hours without smoking a cigarette, and you said, 'That's impossible,' that would mean that you're addicted to nicotine. Similarly, if you can't go for twenty-four hours without saying unkind words about others, then you've lost control over your tongue."

At this point, I almost always encounter the same objection: "How can you compare the harm done by a bit of gossip or a few unpleasant words to the damage caused by alcohol and smoking?"

Is my point overstated? Think about your own life: Unless you, or someone dear to you, have been the victim of terrible physical violence, chances are the worst pains you have suffered in life have come from words used cruelly—from ego-destroying criticism, excessive anger, sarcasm, public and private humiliation, hurtful nicknames, betrayal of secrets, rumors and malicious gossip.

Yet—wounded as many of us have been by unfairly spoken words—when you're with friends and the conversation turns to people not present, what aspects of their lives are you and your companions most likely to explore? Is it not their character flaws and the intimate details of their social lives?

If you don't participate in such talk, congratulations. But before you assert this as a definite fact, monitor yourself for the next two days. Note on a piece of paper every time you say something negative about someone who is not present. Also record when others do so too, as well as your reactions to their words when that happens. Do you try to silence the speaker, or do you ask for more details?

To ensure the test's accuracy, make no effort to change the contents of your conversations throughout the two-day period, and don't try to be kinder than usual in assessing others' character and actions.

Most of us who take this test are unpleasantly surprised.

Negative comments we make about those who are absent is but one way we wound with words; we also often cruelly hurt those *to whom* we are speaking.[1] For example, many of us, when enraged, grossly exaggerate the wrong done by the person who has provoked our ire. If the anger we express is disproportionate to the provocation (as often occurs when parents rage at children), it is unfair, often inflicts great hurt and damage, and thus is unethical. Similarly, many of us criticize others with harsh and offensive words, or cannot have a dispute without provoking a quarrel. Others of us are prone to belittle or humiliate other people, even in public. This is an evil of such profound magnitude and consequence that Jewish law questions whether anyone who is guilty of this offense can ever fully repent.

One reason that many otherwise "good" people often use words irresponsibly and cruelly is that they regard the injuries inflicted by words as intangible and, therefore, minimize the damage they can inflict. Thus, for generations, children taunted by playmates have been taught to respond, "Sticks and stones can break my bones, but words [or names] can never hurt me."[2]

In our hearts, we all know that this saying is untrue. The National Committee for Prevention of Child Abuse has compiled a list of disparaging comments made by angry parents to children, including:

"You're pathetic. You can't do anything right."
"You disgust me. Just shut up!"
"Hey, stupid. Don't you know how to listen?"
"You're more trouble than you're worth."
"Get outta here. I'm sick of looking at your face."
"I wish you were never born."

Does anybody really believe that a child raised with such abuse believes that "sticks and stones can break my bones, but words [or names] can never hurt me"?

An old Jewish teaching compares the tongue to an arrow. "Why not another weapon, a sword, for example?" one rabbi asks. "Because," he is told, "if a man unsheathes his sword to kill his friend, and his friend pleads with him and begs for mercy, the man may be mollified and return the sword to its scabbard. But an arrow, once it is shot, cannot be returned, no matter how much one wants to."[3]

The rabbi's comparison is more than a metaphor. Because words can be used to inflict devastating and irrevocable suffering, Jewish teachings go so far as to compare cruel words to murder. A penitent thief can return the money he has stolen; a murderer, no matter how sincerely he repents, cannot restore his victim to life. Similarly, one who damages another's reputation through malicious gossip, or who humiliates another publicly, can never fully undo the damage.

As powerful as the capacity of words to hurt is their ability to heal and inspire. The anonymous author of a medieval Jewish text, the *Orhot Tzaddikim* (*The Ways of the Righteous*), spends pages warning of the great evils routinely committed in speech. "With the tongue one can commit numerous great and mighty transgressions such as informing, talebearing, mockery, flattery and telling lies," *but,* he reminds his readers, "with the tongue, one can also perform limitless acts of virtue."

Recently, I witnessed this principle at work in my own family. One day, our five-year-old daughter Naomi was in a weepy mood, and in a moment of frustration, my wife, Dvorah, yelled at her, "I hate it when you keep crying over nothing! It hurts my ears. If you can't stop crying, I will have to leave you at home!"

The next morning at breakfast, Shira, Naomi's three-year-old sister, started crying. Naomi stuffed both index fingers in her ears, and screamed at her sister: "I hate it when you cry! It hurts my ears. If you have to cry, go into the other room."

Dvorah was dumbstruck. Naomi had exactly replicated her impatient tone, her chiding, even some of her words. Embarrassed, and eager to show Naomi a better response, she went over to the crying Shira, sat her on her lap, and said, "Mommy's sorry she forgot to wait for you to add the blueberries to the pancakes. I never want to make you cry. I'm just going to sit by you until all baby Shira's tears go away."

Naomi carefully studied this exchange, and during the coming days and weeks, Dvorah made a point of repeating such compassionate reassurance whenever she saw Naomi or any of our other children crying.

Some time later, our youngest child, two-year-old Benjamin, kicked Shira, prompting a fit of wailing. This time Naomi sat down beside her hurt sister and said comfortingly, "It's okay, Shira. No more crying. I'm going to sit right here for the whole night and wait for you to stop."

Dvorah and I learned as valuable a lesson as Naomi from this incident, one that had been expressed about a century earlier by the Haffetz Hayyim, a great Eastern European rabbinic scholar. He once taught: "When people are preparing a telegram, notice how carefully they consider each word before they put it down. That is how careful we must be when we speak."

PART
ONE

The Unrecognized Power of Words

1

The Unrecognized
Power of Words

In a small Eastern European town, a man went through the community slandering the rabbi. One day, feeling suddenly remorseful, he begged the rabbi for forgiveness and offered to undergo any penance to make amends. The rabbi told him to take a feather pillow from his home, cut it open, scatter the feathers to the wind, then return to see him. The man did as he was told, then came to the rabbi and asked, "Am I now forgiven?"

"Almost," came the response. "You just have to do one more thing. Go and gather all the feathers."

"But that's impossible," the man protested. "The wind has already scattered them."

"Precisely," the rabbi answered. "And although you truly wish to correct the evil you have done, it is as impossible to repair the damage done by your words as it is to recover the feathers."

This famous tale is a lesson about slander, of course, but it also is a testimony to the power of speech. Words said about us define our place in the world. Once that "place," our reputation, is defined—particularly if the definition is negative—it is very hard to reverse. President Andrew Jackson, who, along with his wife, was the subject of relentless malicious gossip, once noted, "The murderer only takes the life of the parent and leaves his character as a goodly heritage to his children, while the slanderer takes away his goodly reputation and leaves him a living monument to his children's disgrace."

The Jewish tradition views words as tangible (in Hebrew, one of the terms for "words" is *devarim,* which also means "things"), and extremely powerful. The Bible clearly acknowledges the potency of words, teaching that God created the world with words. As the third verse of Genesis records: "And God said, 'Let there be light,' and there was light."

Like God, human beings also create with words. We have all had the experience of reading a novel and being so moved by the fate of one of its characters that we felt love, hate, or anger. Sometimes we cried, even though the individual whose fate so moved us never existed. All that happened was that a writer took a blank piece of paper, and through words alone created a human being so real that he or she was capable of evoking our deepest emotions.

That words are powerful may seem obvious, but the fact is that most of us, most of the time, use them lightly. We choose our clothes more carefully than we choose our words, though what we say *about* and *to* others can define them indelibly. That is why ethical speech—speaking fairly of others, honestly about ourselves, and carefully to everyone—is so important. If we keep the power of words in the foreground of our consciousness, we will handle them as carefully as we would a loaded gun.

Unfair speech, however, does more than harm its victim; it also is self-destructive. Psychiatrist Antonio Wood notes that when we speak ill of someone, we alienate ourselves from that person. The more negative our comments, the more distant we feel from their object. Thus, one who speaks unfairly of many people, comes to distance and alienate himself from many individuals, and, as Dr. Wood notes, alienation is a major cause of depression, one of the most widespread and rapidly growing disorders in America.

The avoidance of alienation is but one way in which one can benefit from avoiding unethical speech. People who minimize the amount of gossip in which they engage generally find that their connections to others become more intimate and satisfying. For many, exchanging information and opinions about other people is an easy, if divisive, way of bonding with others. But those who refrain from gossiping are forced to focus more on themselves and the person to whom they are speaking. The relationship established thereby almost invariably is emotionally deeper.

In addition, anyone who makes an effort to speak fairly to others and to avoid angry explosions finds that his social interactions become smoother. Admittedly, when one is angry at someone, maintaining a good relationship with that individual might seem irrelevant. But consider—particularly if you have a quick temper—whether you've ever heard yourself say, "I don't care if I never speak with him [or her] again!" about someone with whom you are now friendly. People who learn to speak fairly avoid going through life regretting cruel words they said, and friendships needlessly ended.

In the larger society too, we are in urgent need of more civilized discourse. Throughout history, words used unfairly have promoted hatred and even murder. The medieval Crusaders didn't wake up one morning and begin randomly killing Jews. Rather, they and their ancestors had been conditioned for centuries to think of Jews as "Christkillers" and thus less than human. Once this verbal characterization took hold, it became easy to kill Jews.

African Americans were long branded with words that depicted them as subhuman ("apes," "jungle bunnies," "niggers"). The ones who first used such terms hoped they would enable whites to view blacks as different and inferior to themselves. This was important because if whites perceived blacks as fully human, otherwise "decent" people could never have arranged for them to be kidnapped from their homes, whipped, branded, and enslaved.

Similarly, when the radical Black Panther party referred to police as "pigs" during the 1960s, its intention was not to hurt policemen's feelings, but to dehumanize them and thereby establish in people's minds that murdering a policeman was really killing an animal, not a human being.[1]

Unfair, often cruel, speech continues to poison our society. Rush Limbaugh, the country's most popular talkshow host, repeatedly labels those feminists he regards as radically pro-choice as "feminazis," leading listeners to believe that there is a significant body of feminists (if they are not significant, why is Limbaugh bothering to attack them?) who think like Hitler and plan, like the Nazis, to do horrible things to those who oppose them. To call Gloria Steinem and Bella Abzug "feminazis," as Limbaugh does, is unethical, makes rational discourse impossible, and constitutes an unintentional mockery of the sufferings of the Nazis' real victims.[2] G. Gordon Liddy, another right-wing talk-show host, and a man who has been highly honored within his industry, advises his listeners to aim for the head rather than the bulletproof vests of invading federal ATF agents.

Verbal incivility characterizes some highly partisan liberals no less than conservatives. When George Bush was elected president in 1988, Mayor Andrew Young and Congressman Richard Gephardt commented that not since the days of Hitler and Goebbels had a political campaign been built so deliberately on the technique of the Big Lie.[3] What an irony! In the very act of condemning Bush's campaign for its supposed lies, Young and Gephardt tell a much bigger and vicious untruth. With similarly overwrought and unethical language, Senator Ted Kennedy reacted to one of President Ronald Reagan's Supreme Court nominations by asserting: "Robert Bork's America is a land in which women would be forced into back alley abortions, blacks would sit at segregated lunch counters, rogue police could break down citizens' doors in midnight raids, school children could not be taught about evolution, [and] writers and artists could be censored at the whim of government."[4] Those familiar with Judge Bork's views and judicial record knew that Kennedy's statement was an amalgamation of untruths and misleading half-truths. But the senator's agenda was neither accuracy nor fairness; it was to defeat Bork's nomination.

In popular culture the deterioration of civilized discourse is even more pronounced than in politics. A contemporary musical genre, "gangsta rap," glorifies killing police and raping women. A 1990 album, *The Geto Boys,* by the group of the same name, includes this horrendous couplet:

I dug between the chair and whipped out the machete
She screamed, I sliced her up until her guts were like spaghetti.

Another lyric in this album speaks of the need to "stab the girl" in her breasts, and "just cut her to bits."[5]

Gangsta rap is only one manifestation of contemporary music's incendiary usage of language. When Axl Rose, lead singer of Guns N' Roses (famous for the lyric "I'll rip your heart in two and leave you lying on the bed"), attended a "homecoming" concert in Indianapolis in 1991, he told his cheering fans that "kids in Indiana today are just like prisoners in Auschwitz."[6] Film critic Michael Medved has commented: "When he later defended these appalling remarks in conversations with reporters, no one thought to ask Rose the obvious question: If he really believes that parents are like guards at a Nazi death camp, wouldn't teenagers be perfectly justified in killing them in order to achieve their freedom?"[7]

If so, one could be sure that some leading figures of the youth culture would be far from upset. Responding to the alarming statistics of black-on-black crime, rap star Sister Souljah suggested that "maybe we should have a week of killing whites. Just give back what whites have done to us."[8]

A nineteenth-century story tells of a man who saw a large sign over a store, PANTS PRESSED HERE. He brought in his pants to be pressed only to be told, "We don't press pants here, we only make signs."

The "sign makers" of our time are those who compare their political opponents or parents to Nazis, and glorify mutilating women; in short, those who use words to incite rather than inform.

Violence, however, is only one possible result of unethical speech. Another is the destruction of what decent people consider their most important possession, a good name. Raymond Donovan, President Reagan's first secretary of labor, was the victim of a long campaign of rumors and innuendo, which finally culminated in a criminal prosecution. After running up legal bills in excess of a million dollars, he was acquitted of all charges. When he emerged from the courtroom, and reporters swarmed around him for his comment, Donovan posed a bitter question: "Where do I go to get my reputation back?"

Truly—as the anguished Ray Donovan knew—once feathers have been scattered to the wind, they cannot all be recovered.

PART
TWO

How We Speak About Others

A gossip always seeks out the faults of people; he is like the flies who always rest on the dirty spot. If a man has boils, the flies will ignore the rest of the body and sit on the boil. And thus it is with a gossip. He overlooks all the good in a man and speaks only of the evil.

—*Orhot Tzaddikim*
(The Ways of the Righteous)

Lashon hara: the whispering campaign that cannot be stopped, rumors it's impossible to quash, besmirchment from which you will never be cleansed, slanderous stories to belittle your professional qualifications, derisive reports of your business deceptions and your perverse aberrations, outraged polemics denouncing your moral failings, misdeeds, and faulty character traits—your shallowness, your vulgarity, your cowardice, your avarice, your indecency, your falseness, your selfishness, your treachery. Derogatory information. Defamatory statements. Insulting witticisms. Disparaging anecdotes. Idle mockery. Bitchy chatter. Malicious absurdities. Galling wisecracks. Fantastic lies. *Lashon hara* of such spectacular dimensions that it is guaranteed not only to bring on fear, distress, disease, spiritual isolation, and financial loss but to significantly shorten a life. They will make a shambles of the position that you worked nearly sixty years to achieve. No area of your life will go uncontaminated. And if you think this is an exaggeration you really *are* deficient in a sense of reality.

—Philip Roth,
Operation Shylock

If you say of a rabbi that he does not have a good voice and of a cantor that he is not a scholar, you are a gossip. But if you say of a rabbi that he is no scholar and of a cantor that he has no voice—you are a murderer.

—Rabbi Israel Salanter

The gossiper stands in Syria and kills in Rome.
>—Palestinian Talmud, *Peah* 1:1

I can retract what I did not say, but I cannot retract what I already have said.
>—Solomon Ibn Gabirol, *Pearls of Wisdom*

Why do human fingers resemble pegs? So that if one hears something unseemly, one can plug one's fingers in one's ears.
>—Babylonian Talmud, *Ketubot* 5b

2

The Irrevocable Damage Inflicted by Gossip

"What does a good guest say? 'How much trouble has my host gone to for me. How much meat he set before me. How much wine he brought me. How many cakes he served me. And all this trouble he has gone to for my sake!' But what does a bad guest say? 'What kind of effort did the host make for me? I have eaten only one slice of bread. I have eaten only one piece of meat, and I have drunk only one cup of wine! Whatever trouble the host went to was done only for the sake of his wife and children.' "[1]

These two takes on the same party, reported in the Talmud nearly two thousand years ago, go straight to the heart of ethical speech: the fact that most of us, given a willing ear, are bad guests and, often, disloyal friends. It is

15

infinitely more interesting to look for others' flaws—in the case just cited, the supposed self-interest of our host—than to praise their good qualities. How much more satisfying it is to chew over the fact that so-and-so is having an affair, was fired from his job for incompetence, has filed for bankruptcy or, less seriously, for that matter, tells very unfunny jokes and then laughs at them uproariously, than to discuss how good a spouse, how loyal an employee, how financially circumspect, how wonderful a raconteur he may be.

How strange that dinner parties, where we have partaken of a host's hospitality, so often seem to prompt the most critical "postmortems."*

The impulse to be a "bad guest" violates the biblical injunction "You shall not go about as a talebearer among your people" (Leviticus 19:16). This directive is the foun-

---

*My hunch is that more speculative, and often unkindly, gossip and character analysis are exchanged immediately after people leave a dinner party than at any other time. We speculate during the ride home about our hosts' wealth, marriage relationship, aesthetic sensibilities, taste in food, intelligence, and children's personalities.

It is obvious how very unfair such talk is. I know that when my wife and I invite people over for dinner or a party, we work incredibly hard for many hours, sometimes even several days, to make the evening as pleasant as possible for our guests. It hurts that they might leave, then pass the time driving home sharing often critical observations about us. I don't think I am being paranoid in fearing that this is what many of them do; regretfully, I realize how often I have done so myself.

When leaving the home of those who have tried to provide us with a pleasant evening, the simplest and fairest rule to follow is to say nothing disparaging about them. If you find that you are incapable of abiding by this rule, at least don't speak negatively during the ride home. Hold off for a day; perhaps when you finally make your comments, they will be toned down. Before saying anything, think about the effort these people expended to make the gathering pleasant, and ask yourself if it is appropriate to respond with critical observations.

Few things seem more unjust than partaking of other people's hospitality, thanking them, and then, like a spy, utilizing information you acquired in their home to cut them down. If you think that your comments about others are rarely malicious, then ask yourself if you would be willing to make the same remarks directly to your host and/or hostess. If the answer is no, then why communicate them to others?

dation of Jewish dictums on ethical speech—which, not coincidentally, appears only two verses before the Bible's most famous law: "Love your neighbor as yourself" (Leviticus 19:18).

Because the biblical commandment is so terse, it is difficult to know exactly what is meant by "talebearing." Does it mean that you are forbidden to talk about any aspect of other people's lives (telling a friend, "I was at a party at so-and-so's house last night. It's absolutely gorgeous what they've done with their kitchen")? Or does the verse only outlaw damning insinuations ("When Sam went away on that business trip last month, I saw his wife, Sally, at a fancy restaurant with this very good-looking guy. She didn't see me, because they were too busy the whole time making eyes at each other")? Is it talebearing to pass on true stories ("Sally confessed to Betty she's having an affair. Sam ought to know what goes on when he's out of town")?

The Bible itself never fully answers questions of this nature. But starting with the early centuries of the Common Era, Jewish teachers elaborated upon the biblical law and formulated, in ascending order of seriousness, three types of speech that people should decrease or eliminate:

1. Information and comments about others that are nondefamatory and true

2. Negative, though true, stories (in Hebrew, *lashon ha-ra*)—information that lowers the esteem in which people hold the person about whom it is told. A subdivision of this is tattling (in Hebrew, *rechilut*)—telling Judy, for example, the critical things Ben said about her.

3. Lies and rumors (in Hebrew, *motzi shem ra*)—
statements that are negative and false

NONDEFAMATORY AND TRUE REMARKS

The comment "I was at a party at so-and-so's house last night. It's absolutely gorgeous what they've done with their kitchen" is nondefamatory and true. What possible reason could there be for discouraging people from exchanging such innocuous, even complimentary, information?

For one thing, the listener might not find the information so innocuous. While one person is describing how wonderful the party was, the other might well wonder, "Why wasn't I invited? I had them over to my house just a month ago"; or "Funny that they had the money to redo their kitchen since they pleaded poverty when I asked them to contribute to the new hospice."

The more important reason for discouraging "innocuous" gossip is that it rarely remains so. Suppose I suggest that you and a friend spend twenty minutes talking about a mutual acquaintance. How likely is it that you will devote the entire time to exchanging stories about her niceness?

Maybe you will—that is, if the person about whom you're speaking is Mother Teresa. Otherwise, the conversation will likely take on a negative tone. This is because, for most of us, exchanging critical evaluations about others is far more interesting and enjoyable than exchanging accolades. If I were to say to you, "Janet is a wonderful person. There's just *one thing* I can't stand about her," on what aspects of Janet's personality do you think the rest of our conversation will most likely focus?

Even if you don't let the discussion shift in a negative direction, becoming an ethical speaker forces you to anticipate the inadvertent harm that your words might cause. For example, although praising a friend might seem like a laudable act, doing so in the presence of someone who dislikes her will probably do your friend's reputation more harm than good. Your words may well provoke her antagonist to voice the reasons for his dislike, particularly if you leave soon after making your positive remarks.

Strangely enough, the Bible depicts God as causing terrible damage to a righteous man by praising him in his enemy's presence. As the book of Job opens, God is surrounded by angels, among them Satan, who informs God that he has been roaming the earth. The Lord asks Satan, "Have you noticed my servant Job? There is no one like him on earth, a blameless and upright man who fears God and shuns evil."

Satan accuses God of being naive: "Does not Job have good reason to be God-fearing? Why, it is You who has put a fence around him and his household and all that he has. You have blessed his efforts so that his possessions spread out in the land. But lay Your hand upon all that he has and he will surely blaspheme You to Your face" (Job 1:9–11).

Certain that Job will remain loyal to Him no matter what the provocation, the Lord permits Satan to do anything to Job except take his life. In short order, Satan arranges to have Job's ten children killed, his possessions destroyed, and Job himself afflicted with terrible maladies. Although the Book of Job has a happy ending, would anyone dispute that Job's life would have proceeded far more smoothly had God not chosen to praise him before Satan?

The danger of praise leading to damage is at the root of the Book of Proverbs' rather enigmatic observation: "He who blesses his neighbor in a loud voice in the morning, it will later be thought a curse" (27:14).

Bible commentaries understand this to mean that if a person comes to public notice even as a result of a neighbor's "blessing" (a positive association), the intense scrutiny engendered by his newfound fame ultimately will probably damage his good name—or worse.

Such was the fate that befell Oliver Sipple, an ex-Marine who saved the life of President Gerald Ford in 1975. While Ford was visiting San Francisco, Sipple saw Sara Jane Moore, who was standing next to him, aim a gun directly at the president. Sipple grabbed Moore's arm and deflected her aim so that the bullet missed the president; overnight, he became a national hero.

When reporters came to interview Sipple, he had only one request: "Don't publish anything about me." Unfortunately, his plea piqued the journalists' curiosity; within days, the *Los Angeles Times,* quickly followed by dozens of other newspapers, trumpeted the news that Sipple was active in gay causes in the San Francisco area.

One reporter confronted Sipple's mother in Detroit and asked her what she knew about her son's apparent homosexuality. Mrs. Sipple was visibly stunned, since she had known nothing about it. Of course, that was the reason Sipple had begged reporters not to write about his life. Shortly thereafter, his mother stopped speaking to him. When she died four years later, his father informed Sipple that he wouldn't be welcome at her funeral.

Devastated by the rupture in his relationship with his family, Sipple began to drink heavily, and became increasingly withdrawn from those around him. A few years later, he was found in his apartment, dead at age forty-seven.

The *Los Angeles Times* reporter who publicized Sipple's homosexuality made this postmortem comment: "If I had to do it over again, I wouldn't."[2]

But why did he, and the other reporters, have to do it in the first place? Sipple had saved the life of the president; the entire country was deeply in his debt. Yet the insatiable curiosity of the press (and readers) to learn the "true story" about this new American hero caused them to search for a fresh angle. After all, how many times could they describe how he had caused Moore's gun to misfire? His action, while very heroic, became somewhat boring after two or three tellings.[3]

The Sipple case demonstrates the inadvertent damage that can be done even when people start out talking positively about others. *Unless we remain acutely conscious of the direction in which a conversation is heading, such talk is unlikely to remain innocuous.*

"NEGATIVE TRUTHS" (*LASHON HA-RA*)

As a rule, most people seem to think that there is nothing morally wrong in spreading negative information about others as long as the information is true. Jewish law takes a very different view. Perhaps that is why the Hebrew term *lashon ha-ra** has no precise equivalent in English. For unlike slander, which is universally condemned as immoral because it is false, *lashon ha-ra* is by definition true. It is

*Literally, "bad language" or "bad tongue."

the dissemination of *accurate* information that will lower the status of the person to whom it refers; I translate it as "negative truths." Jewish law forbids spreading negative truths about anyone unless the person to whom you are speaking needs the information (for examples of when and to whom such information should be revealed, see pages 28 and 46–54). It is a very serious offense, one that has been addressed by many non-Jewish ethicists as well. Two centuries ago, Jonathan K. Lavater, a Swiss theologian and poet, offered a still apt guideline concerning the spreading of such news: "Never tell evil of a man if you do not know it for a certainty, and if you know it for a certainty, then ask yourself, 'Why should I tell it?' "*

Intention has a great deal to do with the circumstances in which it is prohibited to speak negative truths. The same statement, depending on the context, can constitute a compliment, gossip of the nondefamatory sort, or the more serious sin of *lashon ha-ra*. For example, if you say that a person known to have limited funds gave a hundred dollars to a certain charity, this would probably raise the person's stature because people will be impressed at his generosity. But if you say that a wealthy individual gave a hundred dollars to the same cause, the effect will be to diminish respect for her; she will now be thought of as

*The *fairness* of disseminating negative information is a particularly important but frequently overlooked criterion by people who gossip. I often ask lecture audiences: "How many of you can think of at least one episode in your life that would cause you great embarrassment were it to become known to everyone else here?"

Usually, almost every hand goes up except those who have poor memories, or who have led exceptionally boring lives, or are lying. I suspect that most people who raise their hands are not concealing a history of armed robbery. Nevertheless, were a particularly embarrassing episode known to the public, it might disproportionately influence others' impressions of that person. Because such information would probably be unusual, it might even become the primary association other people have with the person, which of course is the very reason he or she wants it kept private. Thus, although such information is true, disseminating it would be unfair.

miserly. Such a statement, therefore, is *lashon ha-ra;* it might be true, but it lowers respect for the person and is no one else's business.

Unfortunately, this doesn't deter many people from speaking negative truths. Such gossip is often so interesting that it impels many of us to violate the Golden Rule, "Do unto others as you would have others do unto you." Although we would probably want similarly embarrassing information about ourselves to be kept quiet, many of us refuse to be equally discreet concerning others' sensitive secrets.

The injunction against *lashon ha-ra* does not only apply to the use of words. Making a face when someone's name is mentioned, rolling one's eyes, winking, or saying sarcastically, "So-and-so is very smart" are all violations of the law. Since *lashon ha-ra* is considered anything that lowers another person's status, it is irrelevant whether one uses a nonverbal technique to commit it. Jewish law designates this behavior *avak lashon ha-ra* (the "dust of *lashon ha-ra*").

Other examples of such "dust" include innuendo—"Don't mention Paula's name to me. I don't want to say what I know about her." It is equally wrong to imply that there is something derogatory about a person's earlier life: "Who of us who knew Jonathan years ago would have guessed that he would achieve the success he has now?"

The "dust of *lashon ha-ra*" encompasses a whole range of stratagems by which people sometimes damage reputations without saying anything specifically critical. For example, it is morally wrong to show someone a letter you have received that contains spelling mistakes if all you wish to do is cause the reader to have a diminished respect for the letter writer's intelligence.

WHEN GOSSIP IS FALSELY
ATTRIBUTED TO YOU

If a rumor circulates that you said something unkind about someone, and it isn't true, you must make this known both to the person involved and to others. If you don't, the person slandered will remain justifiably hurt and angry. Compare the way two different public figures dealt with this situation:

In *Attlee,* a biography of Clement Attlee, British prime minister and longtime adversary of Winston Churchill, author Kenneth Harris notes the following incident: "After the war, one quip which went the rounds of Westminster was attributed to Churchill himself. 'An empty taxi arrived at 10 Downing Street, and when the door was opened, Attlee got out.' When . . . [a friend] repeated this, and its attribution, to Churchill he obviously did not like it. His face set hard, and 'after an awful pause' he said: 'Mr. Attlee is an honorable and gallant gentleman, and a faithful colleague who served his country well at the time of her greatest need. I should be obliged if you would make it clear whenever an occasion arises that I would never make such a remark about him, and that I strongly disapprove of anybody who does.' "[4]

Compare Churchill's disavowal of his cruel, if witty, comment with the behavior of a prominent former congresswoman toward New York's onetime mayor Ed Koch. Unlike Attlee and Churchill, the congresswoman and Koch had long been political allies; in fact, he had campaigned for her when she ran for the U.S. Congress, as she did for him when he ran for City Hall.

However, several years later this woman took a trip

with Mayor David Dinkins to lobby the Democratic party to hold its 1992 convention in New York City. In a newspaper article about the trip, she was quoted as saying that she was happy to be traveling with Dinkins, whereas she would hate the thought of spending a week with Koch. The latter, unaware of any falling out between them, was both incensed and confused.

A few months later, Koch was even more stunned when the woman, launching a run for the U.S. Senate, called him at his law office to solicit his support. In his memoirs, *Citizen Koch*, he records the ensuing conversation:

> "Well . . . ," I said, "it's strange that you should call me, because you are the last person I would support."
>
> "Why do you say that, Ed?" she said. "I thought we were friends."
>
> "I thought so too," I replied. I then reminded her of her remarks from several months back.
>
> "Did I say that?" she said.
>
> "Yes," I said.
>
> "Well, I don't remember ever saying that."
>
> "I have the clipping here at my office," I explained. "I can send you a copy to refresh your memory."
>
> "Well, if I did say it," she allowed, "it must have been taken out of context."
>
> "Did you write a letter to the editor, stating you had been quoted out of context?"
>
> "No."
>
> "Did you call the reporter, or send him a note, seeking a retraction?"

"No."

"Did you call me, to apologize, or offer an explanation?"

"No."

"Then it wasn't out of context," I said.[5]

Koch was right. If you have publicly said something cruel, and regret it, call the victim of your remarks immediately and apologize. You can be sure that the person will have heard about it, and if you don't apologize, he or she has a right to assume that you meant precisely what you said.

If a cruel statement is attributed to you but you didn't make it, even more aggressive action is required, for why should people associate you with cruel words you haven't uttered? Even if others dismiss the ugly words as inconsequential, you can be certain that the person who feels his name was maligned does not. The congresswoman might well have been a long-term friend of Ed Koch, but from the moment Koch learned about her comment, he identified her in his mind with that one statement.

People simply don't forget cruel words directed against them or against someone they love. Should you be accused of having uttered such words, your only hope for making peace is to *deny* them forcefully (and immediately), both privately and publicly if they are untrue, and to *apologize* in the same manner if they are.

TATTLING (*RECHILUT*)

A subdivision of *lashon ha-ra* is tattling, telling others negative comments people have made about them.

Several years ago, when a close friend of mine announced her engagement, her sister repeated a remark
made by their beloved uncle: "Carol's a very sweet girl,
but David is much more accomplished and worldly than
she is. I'm afraid that he's going to get bored with her."

For Carol, whose father had died when she was very
young, her uncle's critical words were devastating. When
she got married, she refused to walk down the aisle with
him, as they had long planned. Today, several years later,
their once warm relationship is almost nonexistent.

Coincidentally, I saw the sister a short time later and
asked her about this incident. The statement just slipped
out, she told me; she had been chatting with Carol, and it
suddenly occurred to her that she should know what their
uncle really thought.

The sister's answer, a standard justification offered by
people who transmit hurtful comments, seems unarguable
in theory: Aren't we entitled to know whether the people
who act warmly in our presence say cutting things when
we are absent? In practice, however, the one small piece
of "truth" transmitted by a gossip often provides a totally
false impression. Once Carol heard her uncle's comment,
she concluded that it constituted his exclusive opinion of
her. After all, Carol's sister hadn't made a habit of repeating
every complimentary observation their uncle had made
about her.

While the uncle's comment may well have been unkind,
in truth almost all of us have said hurtful things about people

we otherwise love dearly. How many of us would appreciate our parents, children, spouses, and friends hearing every remark that we've ever made about them? "I lay it down as a fact," the great seventeenth-century French philosopher Blaise Pascal once wrote, "that if all men knew what others say of them, there would not be four friends in the world." And as Mark Twain once said, "It takes your enemy and your friend, working together, to hurt you to the heart; the one to slander you and the other to get the news to you."

Of course, there are times when it is appropriate to pass on such information. If you hear someone saying that so-and-so is dishonest, and you know this to be false, you should both publicly dispute the statement and warn the person of what is being said about him. However, such extremely damaging statements are the exception. Generally, unless there is a specific, constructive reason to pass on negative comments, you should not do so.

While Jewish ethics generally forbid lying, one is permitted to be less than fully truthful when asked: "What did so-and-so say about me?" If the reply is likely to inspire ill will, you are permitted to fend off the question with a half-truth, omitting the negative comments the original speaker made. If the questioner presses you for more information—"What else did he say?"—you are allowed to answer that the speaker said nothing critical. (The issue of when lying is permitted is discussed in Chapter 11.)

RUMORS

Reporter Bob Woodward, who along with Carl Bernstein broke the story of the Watergate cover-up, is widely regarded as the most prominent investigative journalist in the United States. You would expect such a professional to be acutely aware of the importance of checking sources for legal, not to mention ethical, reasons. But during the 1989 media uproar that greeted Senator John Tower's nomination as secretary of defense, Woodward, operating under a severe deadline for *The Washington Post*,[6] reported the accusation of a retired air force sergeant who claimed to have witnessed Tower publicly drunk and fondling two women at an army base. According to Woodward's article, the man had witnessed Tower touching one woman's breasts and patting the other's buttocks. The article went on to report the sergeant saying that if one of his daughters had been the victim of such lewd conduct, he would have been "sent to Leavenworth"—the implication being that he would have assaulted Tower and been willing to go to prison as a result.

The air force sergeant was the only named witness in the article; Woodward referred to other "informed sources" who allegedly also were aware of the event, but he never specified who they were. Unsurprisingly, his article led many readers to conclude that Senator Tower was both morally and emotionally unfit to be a Cabinet member.

Within a day of Woodward's article, he learned that his "eyewitness" had earlier been dismissed from the air force because of "mixed personality disorders with anti-social, hysterical features." In other words, Woodward's source was a severely disturbed individual who, it appears, had made up the story.

Confronted with this evidence, Woodward responded: "You report what you can get." He added: "And I wish

I had [had] more time on that story to check."[7] But *ethics* dictate that you *don't* report what you can get; you only report stories that you have *overwhelming* reason to believe are true.[8]

The Talmud, as opposed to Woodward, teaches: "If something is as clear as the fact that your sister is forbidden to you as a sexual mate, [only] then say it."[9] In other words, before bandying about words that can destroy another person's reputation, be as careful as if you were holding a loaded gun.

This should be obvious, but many people, not just journalists, deem it morally acceptable to report rumors. This is particularly unfortunate, since so many rumors are both negative and unfair. When was the last time you heard something like, "Hey, did you hear that so-and-so is really a wonderful person?"

The casualness with which so many rumors are spread constitutes yet another violation of the Golden Rule. When we are the subject of an unpleasant rumor, we desperately do whatever we can to quash it. Yet, when someone else is the rumor's subject, many of us spread it, oblivious to the pain we are causing its victim.

Ask most people whether they ever spread malicious lies about others, and they'll respond, "No." But if you spread a negative rumor that turns out to be untrue, you have done exactly that. Believing that your words might possibly be true affords little consolation to the person whose reputation you have damaged.

Unless there is an ethically compelling reason to pass on a rumor (see next section), the best response to it is to follow the advice of the apocryphal book of Ecclesiasticus: "Have you heard something? Let it die with you. Be strong; it will not burst you" (19:10).

HOW TO PASS ALONG A RUMOR WHEN YOU FEEL ETHICALLY OBLIGATED TO DO SO

In those instances when it is morally permissible to pass on a rumor privately (as in the case of a physician rumored to be practicing treatments that are harmful to patients, or a financial adviser whom you have heard has lost a great deal of money for his clients), it is still forbidden to present as definite something you don't know is a fact. When you disclose "facts" that are only hearsay, the damage you inflict may be devastating and irrevocable. Therefore, even where another's safety or well-being mandates that you report a rumor, you must make clear that it *is* a rumor and requires further investigation. In other words, you should say, "I don't know this to be definitely true, but I've heard that so-and-so has made some very risky investments for his clients, and lost considerable amounts of money. I think you should check further into the matter before you invest money with him."

SLANDER (*MOTZI SHEM RA*)

The most grievous violation of ethical speech is the spreading of malicious falsehoods, what Jewish law calls *motzi shem ra,* "giving another a bad name." Consider the following story, which appeared in *USA Today:*

> *A 9-year-old girl falsely accused a substitute teacher of sexual abuse and bribed 10 other kids to do the same, police said Tuesday.*
>
> *The teacher [whose name, although it appeared in the*

article, I'm omitting], 43, was cleared when police uncovered the plot.

[The man] who had been a substitute for about four weeks apparently had difficulty with the class his first day at Fuller Elementary School and sent some students to the office.

The child offered nine girls and a boy $1 each to report that [the teacher] fondled them.

The Cook County State's Attorney got the complaint May 9; investigators interviewed 14 children the next day "and by the end of the day we knew . . . that every allegation was false," says spokesman Andy Knot.

[The teacher] calls the incident "a nightmare. A lot of people were willing to crucify me."[10]

An especially troubling aspect of this story is that none of the ten children to whom the girl offered a bribe seems to have refused it or to have reported her. They all seemed oblivious to the damage they would do their victim. Yet, to destroy somebody's good name is to commit a kind of murder* (in English, the same idea is conveyed through the expression "character assassination").[11]

The most famous biblical example of a *motzi shem ra* is provided in the Book of Esther. In this book, Haman, adviser to the Persian king Ahasuerus, maliciously lies by telling the king that the Jews refuse to obey his laws. Like many liars, Haman is persuasive, and Ahasuerus soon em-

---

*Indeed, many times it has led to murder. In the fourteenth century, during Europe's devastating Black Plague, antisemites and others seeking scapegoats spread the rumor that Jews had caused the plague by poisoning Europe's wells. Within a few months, enraged mobs had murdered tens of thousands of Jews. In this century and the last, similar sorts of rumormongering bigots provoked the lynching murders of many innocent African Americans in the South.

powers him to murder every Jew living in Persia and its 127 provinces (Esther 3:9–15).

Fortunately, Haman's lies are disproved and his genocidal campaign thwarted. Too often, however, the victims of slanderous tongues are not saved. Thus, in Shakespeare's thirty-eight plays, there is no villain more vile than *Othello*'s Iago, whose evil is perpetrated almost exclusively through words.

At the play's beginning, Iago vows to destroy the Moorish general Othello for bypassing him for promotion. Knowing Othello's jealous nature, Iago convinces him that his new wife, Desdemona, is having an affair with another man. The charge seems preposterous, but Iago repeats the accusation again and again, and arranges the circumstantial evidence necessary to destroy Desdemona's credibility. Soon, Othello comes to believe him. In the end he murders his beloved, only to learn almost immediately that Iago's words were false. For Othello, "Hell," as an old aphorism teaches, "is truth seen too late."

A similarly destructive tongue is possessed by Mary Tilford, the twelve-year-old protagonist of Lillian Hellman's 1934 play *The Children's Hour*. A precocious but vicious child, Mary is disciplined by one of her school's headmistresses. Fearful that other of her misdeeds will soon be uncovered, she confides a scandalous "truth" to Mrs. Tilford, her grandmother: The school's two headmistresses are lesbian lovers. Within hours the grandmother has alerted everyone to this "fact," and alarmed parents withdraw their children from the school.

Weeks later, the rumor is finally proven false, but by then the school has been shut down, one headmistress has committed suicide, and the other has broken off her engagement, certain that her fiancé does not fully believe that the rumor is untrue.

The grandmother feels deep remorse over what has happened. A normally moral person, she knows that she made insufficient efforts to establish the rumor's veracity before destroying the lives of two women. At the play's end, she appears at the surviving headmistress's house, willing to do anything to make amends. Of course, there is nothing she can do other than express some ineffective words of contrition.[12]

"Nobody ever gossips about other people's secret virtues," British philosopher Bertrand Russell once noted. What is *most* interesting to *most* of us about other people is their character flaws and private scandals. Therefore, before you spread information or views that will lower the regard in which an acquaintance is held, ask yourself three questions: Is it true? Is it necessary? Is it fair?[13]

3

The Lure of Gossip

A talmudic parable: "In the future, all the world's animals will come together and confront the snake. They will say to him: 'The lion stalks and then eats its prey, the wolf rips apart another animal and eats it. But you, what is the pleasure you derive in poisoning and killing a human being?' The snake will answer: *'And what is the pleasure human beings derive in spreading malicious gossip* [which humiliates and sometimes kills others]? ' "[1]

As a rule, the rationale for wrongful acts is self-interest: Embezzlers wish to make quick money, guilty defendants manufacture alibis to avoid being punished, and thieves break into a house because they desire another's possessions. But gossips—what do they gain by hurting other people's reputations?

Some fifteen hundred years after the Talmud set down this parable, William Shakespeare conveyed a similar bewilderment about slanderers' actions:[2]

Who steals my purse steals trash, . . .
But he that filches from me my good name
Robs me of that which not enriches him
And makes me poor indeed (Othello III, iii, lines 161–165).

Shakespeare's assertion seems unarguable. A person deprived of his good name by a slanderer is surely impoverished, while the slanderer seems to have gained no benefit. Or has he?

In truth, the benefits derived from spreading malicious gossip may be intangible,[3] but they are no less real. *The most important reason we gossip is to raise our status through lowering the status of others.* There's a tremendous psychological gratification in seeing someone else's social status decline.

Few of us are willing to acknowledge the dirty little secret that our motivation in gossiping is so self-serving. Rather, we would have others believe (and perhaps believe ourselves) that we are talebearers only because the intimate details of other people's lives are inherently so interesting. If that is so, why, then, do we almost always restrict gossip to our social equals or superiors? People rarely talk about the intimate details of their cleaning woman's or gardener's life. The only gossip that makes us feel better about ourselves is precisely that which lowers public esteem of those with whom we are in "status competition," our social peers and/or superiors.

The extraordinary public fascination with the unhappy

marriage of England's Prince Charles and Princess Diana reflects a certain cruel pleasure in seeing members of the British royal family "brought down a peg." Beneath the "tsk-tsks" is gratification in learning that a royal heir apparent and his beautiful wife apparently were leading wretchedly unhappy lives.[4] The endless details about "the misery of the rich and famous" seems to make many people feel better about their own lives.

We also derive great enjoyment from seeing a comedown for those who summon us to a morally upright life. Thus, a clergyman caught—or rumored to have been involved—in a scandal, particularly a sexual one, finds himself the subject of particularly nasty and unrelenting gossip. Such talebearing removes a strong moral pressure on us, for if the individual making moral demands of us can be shown not to abide by such demands him- or herself, then this seems to free us from moral responsibility.

In their pathbreaking *Harvard Law Review* article on "The Right to Privacy," Samuel Warren and future Supreme Court Justice Louis Brandeis noted the enticing element in nasty gossip; it appeals "to that weak side of human nature which is never wholly cast down by the misfortunes and frailties of our neighbors."[5] The word "weak" could as easily have been replaced by "malicious" or "sadistic." We might well have other, more elevated personality traits, but our motives for exchanging tidbits about other people's miseries are rarely noble.

Another way we seek to elevate ourselves is by retailing inside information about others, so that we'll be perceived as being "in the know." As Dr. Samuel Johnson observed two centuries ago, "The vanity of being trusted with a secret is generally the chief motive to disclose it."

Does Dr. Johnson's dictum seem overstated? Then consider the following, admittedly unlikely, scenario: The president of the United States chooses you as his confidant. He speaks with you regularly, sometimes several times a day, shares his innermost thoughts, bounces ideas off you, and otherwise solicits your advice. The only condition attached to your relationship is that you are forbidden to tell anyone, ever, about it. The president also will never mention to anyone, either during his time in office or afterward, that he knows you or has ever spoken to you.

For most of us, I suspect, the satisfaction and pleasure of having such access to the president would largely evaporate if we could tell no one, now or in the future, about it. A primary motive for gossiping is to brag to others about our acquaintance with important people and important things; it follows, therefore, that we must also be important.

This motive for gossip is already apparent in children and adolescents. In *You Just Don't Understand: Women and Men in Conversation,* Deborah Tannen cites anthropological and sociological research that concludes that teenage girls are more likely to betray friends' secrets than boys. Why? Among adolescent boys, Tannen explains, status tends to be based on athletic accomplishments, or, perhaps more important, on the ability to prevail in a physical or verbal fight. Among girls, status is linked more to being connected to the "in crowd": ". . . girls get status by being friends with high-status girls: the cheerleaders, the pretty ones, the ones who are popular with boys. If being friends with those of high status is a way to get status for yourself, how are you to prove to others that a popular girl is your friend? One way is to show that you know her secrets, because it is in the context of friendship that secrets are revealed."[6]

Thus, a girl who is not very attractive or popular proves that she rates high status through the very action that indicates that she is an unworthy friend.

The issue, of course, goes far beyond teenagers and the betrayal of secrets. It seems to be universally accepted that we will be regarded as important people if we know interesting gossip with which others are unfamiliar. In his book *Chutzpah* the well-known Harvard law professor Alan Dershowitz tells a story that reveals a fairly typical kind of gossipmonger:

My mother is vacationing at a Jewish hotel in the Catskill Mountains, and is sitting around with a group of older women. One of them hears my mother's name and, without realizing that she is my mother, launches into a discussion of that other Dershowitz, the Harvard professor. "Such a wonderful boy he is, but why did he have to go off and marry that shiksa [non-Jewish woman]? All the smart and successful ones do it, Henry Kissinger, Ted Koppel . . . ? Why?"

My mother, playing dumb, strings along the know-it-all: "How do you know that Dershowitz married a shiksa?"

Mrs. Know-it-all knows: "My son's cousin is his best friend. He was at the church where they had the wedding."

My mother responds: "Well, I heard that he married a Jewish woman."

"So you heard wrong," Mrs. K.I.A. assures my mother. "That's the story his family is putting out, can you blame them?"

> *At this point my mother can't hold back. "Alan Dershow-*
> *itz is my son. I was at the shul [synagogue] where he married*
> *Carolyn Cohen, whose father's name is Mordechai and whose*
> *mother speaks fluent Yiddish. So what do you say about that?"*
>
> *"Oh, I'm so glad it wasn't true!" Mrs. K.I.A. says*
> *in obvious relief, but quickly adding, "How about Henry*
> *Kissinger, is his wife Jewish too?"*[7]

Silly as this case sounds (can you imagine inventing a story that a cousin of yours attended a church wedding that never happened?), it illustrates what Jack Levin and Arnold Arluke, sociology professors at Boston's Northeastern University, accidentally discovered in a study of gossip: that inventiveness is all too common. For their experiment Levin and Arluke—seeking to see how quickly gossip spread among students—had hundreds of flyers printed announcing a wedding ceremony to be performed in front of the Northeastern student union building. The flyer read: "You are cordially invited to attend the wedding of Robert Goldberg and Mary Ann O'Brien on June 6 at 3:30 in the afternoon." They circulated the flyers throughout the campus, tacking them on bulletin boards, stacking them in classrooms, and so on. Robert Goldberg and Mary Ann O'Brien were fictitious figures, and Levin and Arluke distributed the flyers on June 7, the day after the wedding supposedly occurred.

A week later, when they polled students to learn how many had "heard" about the wedding, they discovered that 52 percent had. "More amazingly," they note, "12 percent told us they had actually attended [it]! These students said they were there on June 6; many of them described the 'white wedding gown' worn by the bride and the 'black limo' that drove the newlyweds to their honeymoon destination."[8]

The students' responses seemed so bizarre that the two sociologists checked to see if a campus wedding might have occurred on or about the same time, but none had. In their quest to be perceived as people who had the "inside scoop about the big event," 12 percent of the students polled were willing to tell a flat-out lie. The desire to seem important can impel otherwise rational people to act in a pathetically dishonest way.

How ultimately meaningless such artificial elevation of one's status is. How much more satisfying it is to let one's accomplishments cause others to raise their opinion of us.

Yet a third reason we speak ill of others is to exact revenge against people who have wronged us but whom we are too timid to confront. It's natural to have this impulse, for if we complain to the offending party, we risk being hurt again by her response. We can easily find consolation, as well as justification for our anger, when others share our feelings about the offense and the offender.

This form of gossip usually is particularly unfair. Because we want others to share our anger, we often fail to describe very precisely the offense committed against us. If we did, our complaints might not strike other people as so terrible; they might even think that *we* are at least partially responsible for the dispute. So we exaggerate; we describe people as having said more insulting things than they actually did, or as having acted toward us with far greater insensitivity or contempt than was the case. (Most of us are masters at attributing horrendous motives to people who have hurt us.) Our exaggerations, of which we ourselves might not be fully aware, are aimed at provoking others to validate and share our rage.

How productive is this "quick fix"? While almost all fights seem unavoidable when they happen, many turn out to be quite absurd or petty shortly thereafter. If we have made our anger known to many people, we might later find ourselves too embarrassed to make peace with our adversary, whom we have labeled thoroughly despicable. Then, too, once an adversary hears what we are saying about him, he may become even more hostile than before. He may not only resist making peace, he will probably start spreading his account of the dispute, in which we will undoubtedly emerge as considerably less heroic and victimized. Thus, a dispute initiates a whole cycle of injury.

My advice, particularly if the matter is trivial, is to keep your anger to yourself; left alone, it may soon dissipate. Better yet, confront the person who hurt you (before doing so, it might be wise to hold back your angry response for a few days, so as to allow you to see the matter in a broader perspective). Assuming that your adversary is not a terrible individual (which is unlikely if you have been on somewhat friendly terms until now), you could tell her: "You hurt me by saying or doing this . . ." or "I think it was unfair of you to . . ." This might actually lead to an apology and a reconciliation. Ironically, sometimes we don't confront someone we are angry with because we don't wish to hear an explanation for her behavior, lest it deprive us of the self-righteous pleasure of our rage.

Of course, it's not always possible to confront the person at whom you are furious. If you did this with an unfair boss, for example, you might risk losing your job. With a family member or in-law, a confrontation might provoke an irrevocable break. In such cases, it may be helpful to vent your anger to someone else, provided that you choose a confidant who will calm rather than incite you.* But most of the time, however, gossiping merely intensifies the dispute and lessens the chances of reconciliation.

Making a conscious effort to speak ethically can help us become more emotionally direct and responsible, and less likely to relate petty arguments to large numbers of people; we will learn, rather, to directly confront those whom we feel have mistreated us. Instead of being hapless victims, we come to view ourselves as capable of defending our own interests. This might not be the smallest advantage to be gained from undertaking to speak ethically.

IF YOU ARE GOING TO GOSSIP ANYWAY: TWO GUIDELINES

The preceding section describes just a few of the reasons we speak ill of others, and certainly not all gossip is motivated by the wish to do harm. Human behavior is fascinating, and generally anything that intrigues us we desire to share with others. Even the Talmud, the source of most of

---

*Of course, if you are speaking to a therapist, you should feel free to say whatever you want. For therapy to be effective, it is necessary for a patient to be emotionally open and spontaneous. Besides, damage won't result from what you are saying, since the therapist is forbidden to repeat what you have told him or her. Also, unlike some of your other confidants, the therapist will probably try to show why your response might be disproportionate to the provocation, and thus both unhealthy and unfair.

Judaism's laws of ethical speech, acknowledges that virtually everyone violates these laws at least once a day.[9]

What, then, should you do if it is difficult, perhaps impossible, always to refrain from speaking "negative truths" about others?

I suggest first that you severely limit the number of people with whom you gossip (and severely limit the amount of time you spend in such talk). If you or your partner learn something unusual, possibly negative, about a mutual friend, you will probably relate it to each other, and perhaps one or two close friends. But make sure that you stop there.

This is not an ideal solution, since your close friends may also share the information with close friends of theirs.

My friend Dennis Prager, the essayist and talk-show host, argues that forbidding people from transmitting any and all negative information or opinions about others is not only unrealistic but possibly also undesirable. Dennis once asked me, within the context of a conversation we were having about the troubled marriage of a mutual friend, "How can you say you care about someone, and never talk about them?" Furthermore, he argued, "if you never speak about people with your partner, you're probably not very intimate with each other."

I know a woman whose husband almost never spoke about other people to her. She finally said to him with some exasperation, "So what are we supposed to speak about all the time, the dangers of nuclear reactors and the latest actions of the mayor?" People who are close generally talk to each other about the people in their lives.

Therefore, here's a suggestion: If you're going to gossip (with a small number of people), develop a way of talking about others that is as kindly and fair as you would want others to be when saying things about you that, though true, are not complimentary.

4

When, If Ever, Is It Appropriate to Reveal Information That Will Humiliate or Harm Another?

Jewish law compares spreading humiliating or harmful information to shedding blood, an act which is normally, but not always, wrong.*

One specific case in which you are permitted to transmit "negative truths" is when you are asked for a business reference. As the Haffetz Hayyim (1838–1933), the Eastern European rabbinic sage who was Judaism's preeminent authority on the laws of permitted and forbidden speech, teaches: ". . . if a person wants to take someone into his affairs—for example, to hire him in his business, or go into partnership with him . . . it is permitted for him to go around and ask and inquire from others . . . so as to prevent

*With the exception of absolute pacifists, everyone regards the shedding of blood in self-defense as morally right.

possible loss to himself. And it is permissible for others to reveal even very derogatory information, since the intent is not to harm the prospective employee, but to tell the truth in order to save one's fellow human being from potential harm."[1] Similarly, Jewish law insists that you speak frankly when someone requests your opinion about a prospective employee whom you know to be dishonest or incompetent.

Another instance in which it is permitted to reveal information is to someone who is romantically involved with a person whom you know is inappropriate, or if the boy- or girlfriend is concealing information to which the partner is entitled.

In an important overview of Jewish perspectives on "Privacy," Jewish legal scholar Rabbi Alfred S. Cohen tells of a young man whose friend was seriously dating his neighbor. The man knew that his friend had a health problem, but from conversations with the young woman, he realized that she was unaware of his condition. He asked Rabbi Cohen whether he should disclose this fact to her, or whether this would constitute a violation of Judaism's laws forbidding gossip.[2]

The rabbi ruled that Jewish law *obliged* the young man to pass on this information to the woman since she had the right to know about her boyfriend's medical condition before deciding whether or not to marry him. But, he noted, there is no clear-cut moral or legal guideline about *when* to transmit such information. If the man went around telling every woman whom his friend dated about his illness, his friend's social life would be ruined (as would their friendship). On the other hand, a woman who learns such information *after* she has gotten to know the man's more positive aspects will be in a far better position to judge the illness's significance for herself.

Morally, the best course would be for the young man to emphasize to his friend that he has a moral obligation to inform the woman himself, and even to tell him that if he doesn't do so, the friend will. Only in a case where he won't tell the woman, and where the relationship is clearly serious, should another person inform her.[3] Presumably, the same advice would apply if you knew the person had been unfaithful in a previous marriage, or possessed a very bad temper.

Even in instances when you're permitted to share negative information, you should only reveal that which is *relevant*. Thus, if somebody inquires whether X would make a suitable business partner, you may, indeed *should,* say that X cheated a previous partner or that, in a previous job, X came to work every day at 11 A.M. and went home at 3 P.M.; you should not, however, dredge up a fascinating but irrelevant scandal involving X's marriage.

When disclosing negative information, you should tell precisely what you know, and nothing more. If you exaggerate, you are guilty of slander and, in such a case, it would be morally preferable to say nothing at all.

You also should not disseminate embarrassing or negative information about X to anyone besides those who need it. Otherwise moral people frequently violate this principle. They try to justify spreading negative news to large numbers of people by claiming that some who hear such information might need it in the future (for example, everyone needs to know the reason so-and-so's marriage broke up, since someone who hears the story might some-day date the person).

Occasionally, it *is* morally appropriate to share negative information with many people, for example, if a political candidate has misused his office for personal profit, or if a physician is engaging in treatments that are harmful to patients. In such cases, some people will need this information, either to vote against the dishonest politician or to avoid harmful treatments by the unscrupulous doctor.

The guiding principle for disseminating negative information is when the information's recipient will suffer from a "clear and present danger"—not necessarily a life-threatening one—if he or she doesn't possess these facts.

As noted in Chapter 2, if you are uncertain that what you are passing along is definitely true, then you must say so. In such a case, you are permitted to warn an inquiring would-be business partner, employer, or mate to look into a specific matter, but you must explain that this is what you *heard* said, or that this is what you *suspect*. A simple guideline: If you would not be prepared to swear under oath that a story is true, don't present it as undeniably true.

WHEN, IF EVER, SHOULD CONFIDENCES BE BROKEN?

What about deep, dark secrets confided to a cleric or a psychiatrist? Is it ever appropriate to reveal them? Here the ethical standards of the world and of different religions vary.

Consider an elementary or high school psychologist who learns that a student is using illegal drugs. Should the psychologist inform the child's parents? Over the years, I have posed this question before dozens of audiences. A large majority of listeners responds that the parents should be informed. Since they know that I am a rabbi, when I ask them what they think Jewish law would rule, an even larger majority expresses the conviction that it would *insist* that the parents be informed.

In fact, it is likely that Jewish law would take the opposite view. As Rabbi Alfred Cohen argues,[4] involving the parents might ultimately prove beneficial to the child, but the disclosure of confidential information "might effectively stop other students from confiding in that psychologist and thereby prevent their being treated at all. Furthermore, if psychologists could not be trusted to maintain silence, people in general would stop using them. So the question really is, do psychologists benefit society as a whole? Will divulging secrets endanger the practice of that profession? What would be the net result to society if troubled persons no longer had someone to help them cope with personal problems?"[5]

This is a perfect example of the moral difficulties that ensue when an individual good clashes with a societal good. In this specific case, the rabbi suggests that the larger good of society constitutes a higher value than the possible benefit to one individual.

On the other hand, if the psychologist had good reason to believe that the boy's survival depended on his parents' knowing certain information (as in the case of a child contemplating suicide), ethics would dictate ruling differently.[6]

Consider the tragic case of Tatiana Tarasoff, a University of California at Berkeley student, who was murdered by a man named Prosenjit Poddar because she had rebuffed his romantic advances. After his arrest, it was revealed that Poddar had confided to his psychologist, Dr. Lawrence Moore, his intention to murder Tarasoff when she returned from her summer vacation. The psychologist had taken Poddar's threats so seriously that he informed campus police, who in turn detained Poddar for questioning. However, they released him when he appeared to be acting rationally. At that point, Moore's superior, Dr. Harvey Powelson, directed him to desist from further action regarding the case, so that Moore never contacted Tarasoff to warn her about the danger.

Unaware of what Poddar had confided to his psychologist, the Tarasoff family maintained a cordial relationship with the spurned suitor. Poddar even persuaded Tarasoff's brother to share an apartment with him, and thus was in a position to learn when she returned from her vacation, at which time he murdered her.

Tarasoff's parents successfully sued Drs. Moore and Powelson, as well as the University of California, for concealing life-threatening information from them. The majority of judges ruled that while doctor-patient confidentiality normally must be safeguarded, this privileged relationship should be breached when it puts an innocent person in serious danger.

Yet even so commonsensical a conclusion provoked the ire of dissenting Justice William Clark, who argued that the doctor had acted appropriately in not contacting Tarasoff. Because of the majority ruling, he maintained, patients henceforth would fear that information confided to therapists, including threats, might be disclosed, and thus, treatment of the mentally ill would be greatly impaired.[7]

Even if one rejects Justice Clark's premise that it is preferable to sometimes let an innocent person die rather than violate a patient's confidence, the majority ruling in the Tarasoff case still leaves an open question: How can we reconcile our (and society's) need to have outlets for unacceptable feelings with the need to protect the objects of those feelings? Since many people confide fantasies of violence against other people to their therapists, *when* should a mental health professional disclose these threats to a potential victim and to the police? Always? This would hardly be realistic—or desirable. Most of us have probably exclaimed at some point in our lives: "I could kill him! I really could!" It is usually perfectly clear to both the listener and speaker that the threat is not intended seriously. So, if the therapist has good reason to believe that the person is just venting his feelings, then clearly the patient-therapist confidence should not be broken. Does this guideline place an unfair burden on the therapist, forcing her to decide case-by-case whether a threat is seriously intended?

Perhaps the best way to assess such threats is for the therapist to personalize them, to imagine that the violent sentiments are directed toward himself or toward a loved one. If the therapist feels no trepidation about the threat, then it is very likely—though not certainly—inconsequential. On the other hand, if the therapist feels fearful when personalizing the threat (knowing that she would tell her spouse and children, "If you ever see this person come to the house, don't let him [her] in"), she should be morally obliged to inform the potential victim and the authorities. If personalizing a threat makes it seem more potent to the therapist, so be it. If an error must be made, better it should be made in the direction of saving an innocent life rather than safeguarding a would-be murderer's privacy.[8]

Are the ethics different in the case of clergy-client confidentiality? For example, there is a well-known Catholic canon law that prohibits revelations of any statements made in confession, even when a life is at stake.

Not surprisingly, so uncompromising a position can lead to great moral difficulties. In Alfred Hitchcock's classic film *I Confess,* a man confesses to a priest that he murdered someone, then plants circumstantial evidence implicating the cleric. Although the priest is aware of the killer's identity, he finds himself forbidden to disclose it to the police, even after he becomes the prime suspect, and even after an innocent woman's reputation is destroyed during a thorough and somewhat mean-spirited police investigation.[9]

A similar dilemma lies at the heart of Father William Kienzle's best-selling murder mystery *The Rosary Murders.* Here, a serial killer confesses his crime to a priest, and tells him the reason for his actions.[10] Unlike his counterpart in *I Confess,* the priest doesn't know the anonymous confessor's identity. But he too knows that Catholic law forbids him from informing the police about the confession, or any details he learned during it, lest this information enable them to identify the killer. After painful soul-searching—the thought of innocent people dying bothers him terribly—he concludes: "Should protecting the seal [of confession] cost a priest his life, or another innocent life, no reason was sufficient, no cause important enough to violate that seal."[11]

Jewish law is far less categorical. A test case of the principle of rabbi-client confidentiality occurred in New York in 1979 when a pregnant woman, Miriam D., was stabbed fourteen times with a kitchen knife. She died; her baby, whom the doctors tried to save, died three hours later. The murdered woman's husband later sought out a prominent rabbinic scholar and confessed to being haunted by his wife's death, and by the thought that perhaps he might have stabbed her—though he was unsure whether the murder in his mind was a real memory or a dream.

Subsequent to the meeting with the husband of the

murdered woman, and after reviewing the relevant Jewish sources, the rabbi went to the police. Their investigation revealed that the husband, who was deeply in debt (and implicated in the murder of a diamond dealer), had taken out a large life insurance policy on his wife shortly before she was murdered. After the man was arrested, the rabbi testified as a prosecution witness at his trial, and in May 1980 the man was convicted of the murder of his wife.

At the time, some members of the Jewish community felt that the rabbi had acted unjustly; that, at the very least, he should have informed the killer that his disclosures would not be held in confidence. This objection seems unreasonable, given the man's violent nature and the rabbi's natural fear of the harm he might do to protect his terrible secret.

Then, too, an important biblical principle states: "Do not stand by while your neighbor's blood is shed" (Leviticus 19:16), which Jewish law understands as mandating that one not withhold help or information that can be of life-and-death significance to another person. Important as confidentiality is, it is a less compelling value than saving a person's life or bringing a killer to justice.

While people generally have the right to expect a doctor, psychologist, clergyperson, or lawyer to safeguard their secrets, this right is canceled when a higher good, the protection of innocent life, is concerned.

5

Privacy and Public Figures

S o far, we have discussed the rights of ordinary people
to have their privacy respected. But what about public
figures, especially those we have trusted to lead us? Are
they a special case, or do we have the same ethical obliga-
tions toward them?

Many journalists would consider public figures to be a
special case. As Howard Simons, former managing editor
of *The Washington Post* and a prominent proponent of this
view, puts it: "I don't believe any politician in the United
States ought to have a private life."[1]

Those who share this view argue that *any* activity in
which a person engages can reveal significant information
about his or her character; thus, the voting public has the
right to know it all. This belief is now so ingrained in the
American psyche that many people rarely question, on ei-

ther moral and/or practical grounds, the assertion that anyone who enters public life loses the right to protect himself from public scrutiny.

Yet, is it moral to deny *any* human being, including a public official, a sphere of privacy in which she can act without fear that her actions will be reported to large numbers of people?

I would argue that the answer is no, that it is morally unjustifiable to deny public officials a private life. As professor of philosophy David Nyberg writes in *The Varnished Truth:* "A life without privacy is unthinkable. How could we make love? Reflect or meditate? Write a poem, keep a diary . . . attend to those sometimes highly self-conscious requirements of skin and bowels? . . . Civility itself requires privacy."[2] To deny public figures privacy is to deny them both intimate relationships (which are in large measure defined by the sharing of information that is not shared with others) and an internal life.[3]

But don't such no-holds-barred investigations lead voters to select better-qualified, more ethical candidates? Isn't the evil of even intrusive snooping, therefore, outweighed by a greater good? Again I would answer no. Twenty years of muckraking, much of it centered on candidates' private lives, certainly hasn't led to the election of more capable and/or more honest people; its primary achievement has been to make Americans more cynical and less trusting than ever of their elected leaders.[4]

One feature that characterizes what political scientist Larry Sabato labels "attack journalism"[5] is extensive coverage of public figures' sexual indiscretions, a subject that arouses the greatest amount of popular and journalistic obsession. Yet no evidence suggests that presidents (or other public officials or opinion makers) who have cheated on their spouses have proven less effective or, and this is more significant, less trustworthy than presidents who have been faithful.

Franklin Delano Roosevelt, for example, is widely viewed as the greatest American president of the twentieth century. Yet, Roosevelt had a far from satisfactory sex life with his wife, Eleanor, and entered into a lengthy affair with one of his assistants, Lucy Mercer, who was with him when he died. Despite this character flaw, Roosevelt was an effective president who accomplished much good. One would be hard put to show that whatever flaws he had as chief executive were a result of his extramarital relationship. Had his adultery been publicized, he probably would not have been reelected. Would that have been better or worse for the American people?

Compare Roosevelt with Richard Nixon, who apparently was totally faithful to his wife throughout their marriage. Despite his admirable marital monogamy, Nixon remains the only American president forced to resign from office. In his private life, Nixon may well have been a virtuous monogamist, but that proved to be no guarantee of character in other respects.

Downplaying a president's marital infidelity does not mean that the country's good is more significant than any presidential character failings, but rather that such moral shortcomings should be made public knowledge only if they relate to the job for which the individual is running.

If Roosevelt had been guilty of stealing government funds, that would have been a betrayal of his office, something that the public had a need and right to know. But his private sexual behavior had nothing to do with his performance as president.

In short, *negative information that is related to the person's job performance should be made known; negative information that is unrelated to job performance should not.*

But what about John F. Kennedy, whose extramarital indiscretions were far more widespread than Roosevelt's? Is there more reason to believe that his behavior affected his presidential performance?

The evidence suggests not. Of course, if Kennedy had been public about his adultery, insisting that it was his right to flaunt the breaking of his marital vows, that would have been a different matter. Similarly, if during Kennedy's presidential tenure, his critics had maintained that he seemed to be a lazy chief executive, or was often unavailable to carry out his responsibilities, one could make the case that his sexual philandering interfered with his job performance, and that the public would have had the right to know about it. But such criticism of Kennedy was never offered. On the contrary, he was constantly depicted as exceptionally energetic. There appears to be no reason why the public had to know about his sexual behavior.

There is one instance, however, where Kennedy's sexual activities should have been revealed. Before and while he was president, he had an affair with Judith Exner, who was simultaneously the mistress of Sam Giancana, the boss of the Chicago mob. There is strong circumstantial evidence to suggest that she served as a courier between the two men.[6] As columnist William Safire has written: "The private life of any public figure is nobody's business but his own. . . . But when the nation's Chief Executive receives even a few calls from the *home telephone* of the leader of the Mafia in Chicago, that crosses the line into the public's business."[7]

Even in this case, the significance for the public was not Kennedy's acts of adultery per se, but the indirect relationship he thereby established with a Mafia boss. Thus, it equally would have been the public's right to know of this connection had Exner been a close male friend of both Kennedy and Giancana.

Finally, consider Martin Luther King, Jr., the only American whose birthday has been turned into a national holiday during this century. Reverend King was the leading figure in the civil rights movement, which led to the end of legalized segregation. He also was a spiritual leader par excellence, whose "I have a dream" speech, delivered during the 1963 March on Washington, remains one of the century's most powerful, inspirational assertions of human dignity.

Yet Reverend King's illicit liaisons became widely known after his death in 1968, through the activities of one of the most compulsive snoopers and disseminators of "negative truths" and untrue rumors in American history: J. Edgar Hoover, the longtime head of the FBI. Hoover, who had little affection or respect for blacks,[8] placed a tap in hotel rooms where King was staying, and learned of his amorous liaisons. How could broadcasting such information to the public possibly have been in the interests of national security? What possible greater moral good—greater than our defeat of Jim Crow and jogging the nation's conscience—would have been served?

Although adultery is a serious sin, the evidence seems to show that not only can one be simultaneously a good president and an adulterer, and one can even be a great moral leader, as in the case of Dr. King, and engage in extramarital sex (I am of course not advocating this). As essayist Dennis Prager has argued: "Recent history would show that men who have committed adultery were *more* likely to be great leaders than men who have always been faithful. Now, of course," Prager concedes, "such a conclusion is absurd. But it is no more absurd than concluding that men who have committed adultery are less likely to be good leaders."[9]

Americans have paid a steep price for the media's ongoing obsession with sexual gossip. Most important, it has caused media (and hence public) attention to focus on personal rather than substantive issues. Reporter Steven Roberts has observed that "more ink [was] devoted to Wilbur Mills' exploits with Fanne Foxe [a stripper with whom the congressman had had an affair] than to Wilbur Mills' writing half the tax laws on the books. Does that serve the readers and make sense? Not to me."[10]

While Roberts is correct that this makes no *logical* sense, the reason for the media's oddly skewed priorities is clear to anyone who understands human nature.* Most of us are very interested in others' failings, particularly their sexual peccadilloes. Even when we acknowledge that such curiosity is intrusive, uncouth and even immoral, it is difficult

---

*Ask most voters to prioritize a series of issues, including candidates' sexual behavior, in terms of the national interest, and sexual behavior will rank near the bottom. Announce, however, that a television program investigating a candidate's love life will be broadcast at the same time as a program discussing the candidate's positions on the most pressing issues facing America. Which program do you think will attract more viewers? Obviously, the one on sexual conduct. The reason is not that viewers have deluded themselves into thinking that this topic is more important, but that it interests them more. Perhaps the most unfortunate repercussion of the media's obsession with the private lives of public figures is that it has caused Americans to pay less attention to far more substantive and significant issues.

to suppress it. (Let's say you were in a friend's house, walked into the bedroom, and found your friend's diary open. The first words you saw were: "I had sex yesterday with . . ." Would you have the moral strength and character to close the book?)

Over the years, I have asked dozens of audiences: "How many of you think that the public had the right to know about presidential candidate Gary Hart's 1987 affair with Donna Rice?" (the *Miami Herald*'s revelation of which caused the then Colorado senator to withdraw from the 1988 presidential race). Regularly, between 10 and 20 percent say yes, while well over 60 percent say no.

I address my next question only to the "no" majority: "As an outgrowth of your belief that the public had no right to this knowledge, how many of you refused to read articles about Hart's affair, and turned off your television sets when it was announced that pictures were now going to be shown of the woman with whom Hart had his affair?" Almost everyone laughs at this question and, at most, one or two hands go up.

Those who believe that the public had no moral right to know about Gary Hart's affair but who followed the case avidly are not hypocrites; they are human beings with normal human interests. Almost all negative gossip, particularly about sex, is so inherently interesting that it is very hard to ignore. To draw an analogy: Most married Americans believe in monogamy. But if every time they checked into a hotel, a very attractive member of the opposite sex were waiting for them in their rooms, a great many "confirmed" monogamists would commit adultery. Mercifully, few of us have such temptations.

Beyond criminal abrogations of duty such as embezzling funds or the like, the chief offense for which public officials deserve to be called to account is hypocrisy; for example, does the person engage in conduct he denounces or wishes to see punished in others? Even here, however, caution is advised. A few years back, a friend of mine whose husband holds a high public office called me for advice about an ethical dilemma. She and her husband had learned that a prominent adversary of her husband's political party once conducted an adulterous affair. His mistress had become pregnant, and the man urged her to have an abortion. She did, and he paid for it.

Both of us knew that revealing such information would definitely end the man's political career, given that he had carefully cultivated an image of great moral rectitude. I asked my friend only one question: Does this man currently oppose the right of women to have abortions? If yes, his hypocrisy in arranging an abortion when it suited his interests would be so clear that it seemed to me that this information should be released.

But if he supported a woman's right to have an abortion, I believed that "outing" him for having committed adultery would be immoral: The man's relationship with his wife was intact, and the woman with whom he had an affair had gone on with her life. It was only by the strangest of coincidences that this information had come into my friend's hands. Why destroy a person and humiliate his or her family for committing an act that is nobody else's business?*

---

*Whether a person who has had an abortion or paid for one should be denied the right to oppose others' rights to undergo this procedure likewise hinges on the issue of hypocrisy. A person who would adopt such a position should publicly acknowledge what he has done and explain why he now believes that his earlier action was wrong. Otherwise, the person's behavior is hypocritical, and deserves to be part of the public record.

My friend acknowledged that the adversary supported abortion rights but cited other political stances with which she disagreed, positions on which I concurred with her. However, I maintained that it would be indefensible to reveal his infidelity and the abortion. Much as we dislike somebody, to dig up and disseminate whatever "dirt" we can to destroy him or her would still be wrong.

In short, public figures should not be exempt from the right to privacy that we all enjoy. Except for those aspects of their lives that relate to job performance, they should be able to keep their private lives private. Ironically, the obsession with invading our leaders' private lives has not even achieved the one good one might expect: a deeper knowledge of those whose lives have been investigated. Because candidates are aware that the media treat them like arrested felons—"Anything you say can be used against you"—many confine themselves to banalities when speaking in the presence of journalists. They not inappropriately assume that it's safer to appear bland than to risk making a personal revelation or a statement that can be cited out of context and used to damn them in the future.

Finally, it's likely that such intrusive scrutiny discourages many Americans, some with fine characters, from considering public service. How many among us, if nominated to a political position that would provoke our ideological opponents to ask everyone who has known us: "Tell us the worst thing you know about so-and-so, or the worst thing you have ever heard about him. Tell us the names of anybody you know who dislikes him, so we can speak to them," would willingly undergo such scrutiny, however moral our lives?

Even journalists bent on exposing the feet of clay in every public figure's shoes do not wish to sustain such an indignity. In 1987, Paul Taylor, a *Washington Post* reporter, asked presidential candidate Gary Hart whether he thought that adultery was immoral. When Hart said yes, Taylor asked him if he had committed adultery. After a moment's stammering, Hart responded: "I don't have to answer that." A few weeks later, after Hart had withdrawn from the presidential campaign, *People* magazine posed to Taylor the same two questions he had addressed to Hart. "Yes, I do consider adultery immoral," the journalist responded. "The answer to the second question is 'None of your business.' "[11]

In other words, even those who spread gossip don't want to be its victims.* The time has come to return to some of the civility that prevailed in the past.

Perhaps the worst repercussion of "attack journalism" is that some decent people, precisely because they are more

---

*Indeed, many journalists routinely declare their own lives "off limits," even when one could make a case that the public has a legitimate right to know about them. For example, journalists who cover the U.S. Congress or the White House seldom say what political party they belong to or the candidates for whom they voted. But shouldn't the public have the right to know if someone reporting a scandal or other negative information about a candidate or a nominee has previously supported that candidate's opponent? We could then better assess whether the journalist similarly reports negative information about the candidate or party whom he or she supports.

In a parallel situation, *The Washington Post* reports the honoraria paid senators and congressmen by groups before whom they have lectured; it does not, however, report the far larger honoraria paid prominent newspeople for their lectures. Yet, is it unfairly cynical to assume that a journalist covering an organization might be influenced if he has been paid $15,000 or more by that organization for a talk?

easily ashamed, have been and will be discouraged from entering the public arena. *New York Times* columnist Anthony Lewis seems correct in arguing that "if we tell people there's to be absolutely nothing private left to them, then we will tend to attract to public office only those most brazen, least sensitive personalities."[12]

Surely such an outcome serves no moral good.

PART
THREE

How We Speak to Others

6

Controlling Rage and Anger

Only God can give us credit for the angry
words we did not speak.
—Rabbi Harold Kushner,
When All You've Ever Wanted Isn't Enough

T he Bible almost always describes romantic love from
the male's perspective. We are told that Isaac loved
Rebecca (Genesis 24:67), Jacob loved Rachel (Genesis
29:18), and Samson loved Delilah (Judges 16:4). In the
entire Bible there is only one woman whose love for a
man is recorded: "Now Michal, daughter of [King] Saul
had fallen in love with David" (I Samuel 18:20). A short
time later, when Michal's father, afraid that David would
usurp the throne, plotted to kill him, she helped David

escape by lowering him from a window. She then confused the hired assassins by placing a human image, topped with hair and dressed in clothes, in David's bed (I Samuel 19:11–17). By the time the would-be killers realized Michal's ruse, her beloved was far away.

Although the Bible never reports that David reciprocated Michal's love, we do know that he risked his life in one-on-one battle with two hundred Philistines to win Michal's hand in marriage (I Samuel 18:25–29). Later, when David spent years hiding from King Saul, Saul married off Michal, still David's wife, to a man named Phalti. Although many husbands would have repudiated a wife who had acquiesced to such an arrangement, when David became king, he restored Michal as his queen.

Yet, despite the intense love at their relationship's outset, David and Michal's marriage becomes perhaps the saddest in the Bible, and within a few years this once devoted couple were totally estranged. David and Michal both suffered from the same character flaw—a sharp tongue, which they refused to control when angry. The Bible describes the incident that triggered the end of their love. Ironically, it was a celebration: David was supervising the return to Jerusalem of the Ark of the Lord (the holiest object in ancient Jewish life), which the Philistines had captured many years earlier. In an outburst of joy, he danced passionately, even wildly, in front of thousands of his subjects. Watching the whole scene from a palace window, Michal was disgusted by the spectacle of a monarch carrying on with such abandon. And so when David returned to the palace, she greeted him with cold sarcasm: "Didn't the king of Israel do himself honor today—exposing himself . . . as one of the riffraff might expose himself?" (II Samuel 6:20).

Were Michal's withering remarks justified? Had David truly acted in a manner that diminished the dignity of his office? Perhaps, but whether or not Michal was right, her tactless criticism of her husband on this great day in his life blew a dispute into a gale-force fury.

Michal's attack, however, was only the first factor in the tragedy that ensued. In the face of his wife's scorn, David did not remain silent, walk away until the tension eased, or even try to defend his behavior. Instead, he responded with the cruelest counterattack he could muster: "It was before the Lord Who chose me instead of your father and all his family [that I danced]."

David's words in no way addressed the substance of Michal's critique. As many of us do when criticized, he went "straight for blood," attacking the most painful event in Michal's life, God's rejection of her father, and his subsequent death, along with three of Michal's brothers, at the hands of the Philistines.

In the very next verse, the Bible records: "So to her dying day Michal, daughter of Saul, had no children." Why is Michal's childlessness recorded at this point? Perhaps because after so brutal an exchange—and there might well have been others—Michal and David were never again intimate.

The Bible's point is as clear today as it was in 1000 BCE: If a husband or wife, or two siblings or friends, do not restrain their words when they are angry, love is unlikely to survive, *no matter how deeply the two people once cared for each other*. The ability to control what we say when we're angry is a prerequisite for a lasting relationship.

Unfortunately, this piece of biblical wisdom flies in the face of much modern thinking. Today, many people believe that it's unhealthy to suppress rage. If you feel an emotion, it's considered important that you say exactly what you're feeling.

This sort of pop-psychology assertion can be deflated with a one-word question: "Why?"

That you feel rage does not entitle you to inflict emotional pain on others any more than feelings of sexual attraction entitle you to rape the source of your attraction.

Some might argue that, unlike rape, rage is justifiable. Then again, what angry person doesn't feel that his or her rage is justified? One of anger's insidious qualities is that one can find a thousand excuses for it. And while rage sometimes *is* justified—what other emotion should one feel toward an Adolf Eichmann or a Charles Manson?—many of us express it when only far milder emotions are warranted.

As psychotherapist Bernie Zilbergeld has written: "I cannot count the number of times that married couples tell me, 'I've got all this anger bottled up and I need to get it out.' Sure you do, and I'll be happy to cater the divorce."

Even when anger is justified, all that it justifies is expressing anger proportionate to the provocation. If it is disproportionate, it is unfair, unjust, and hence morally wrong.

So what if you find it painful to hold in your angry feelings? Isn't it morally preferable that you experience the pain of suppressing your anger than the person with whom you're angry experience the pain of being on the receiving end?

Rage, however, is not only destructive (as in the case of David and Michal) but also *self*-destructive. The Rabbis claim that when a wise man loses control of his temper, his wisdom deserts him. Thus, the Book of Numbers describes an episode in which Moses becomes outraged at the Israelites' incessant whining about water. God directs him to speak to a large rock, from which He will then send water to satisfy the people's thirst. But Moses, still furious at the Israelites' many years of complaining, disobeys God's command. Instead of speaking to the rock, Moses strikes it, saying, "Listen, you rebels, shall we get water for you out of this rock?" (Numbers 20:10).

Many of us hit objects when angry. The Torah's point is profound: When angry, you should attempt to speak, not hit or burst out in rage. Furthermore, during anger, we are apt to make extreme and unwise comments. Thus, although Moses surely did not intend it, the "we" implied that it was he and Aaron, not God, who were responsible for the miracle of the water gushing forth from the rock. His was a dangerously foolish comment, the kind we all make when angry, which could have led the Israelites to believe that Moses himself was a god.[1] Moses paid dearly for his loss of self-control: God denied him entry into the Promised Land.

In addition to acting unwisely, losing our temper often makes us *appear* foolish. In his book *Acting in Film,* actor Michael Caine recalls that "I used to lose my temper. I would fly off the handle quite quickly in a work situation. Then I worked on a picture called *The Last Valley* by James Clavell, who had been a prisoner of the Japanese during World War II. James looks like an Englishman, but he really thinks like a Japanese. I lost my temper one day, and James just looked at me and let me finish ranting and raving, and then he said, 'Come with me, Mike. Let's go round the corner and sit down.' He sat me down and talked to me about the Japanese theory of losing face . . . if you start to scream and shout, you look like a fool, and you feel like a fool, and you earn the disrespect of everyone. . . . I've never lost my temper in a work situation again."[2]

A close friend of my wife, a man who has long struggled with his temper, once put it: "Haven't you learned already that when you lose control of your temper, you look deranged?"

So it is important to control our rage, however "righteous" it may be. Human beings may well have little control over what *provokes* their anger, *but all of us,* unless we are under the influence of mind-altering drugs, or suffer some mental illness, or have certain types of brain damage, *usually* can control how we express our anger.

Psychologist Richard Gelles tells of a marriage counselor who was interviewing a man who often physically abused his wife. " 'Why do you beat up your wife?' the counselor asked the husband.

" 'I can't control myself,' the man responded. 'I just lose control.'

"The counselor, being a very wise person, asked: 'Well, why don't you shoot her or stab her?'

"The husband had no response to that because the only answer he could have given would be, 'I can't shoot or stab my wife, I might [permanently] hurt her.' [This man] knew very well what he was doing."[3]

If you believe that you truly can't control your temper, imagine the following scenario: You and another person (say, a family member) are having a screaming, no-holds-barred fight when suddenly the doorbell rings. Someone whom you're very eager to impress (a boss or a new client) stands in front of your door. Would you go on ranting or would you find a way to suppress your rage?[4]

Perhaps you would suppress your rage for a short while, for as long as it took the visitor to leave, whereupon the fight would erupt again. But even if that happens, your ability to delay the rage means that you do have some control over your temper. Furthermore, the delay itself would likely lessen the fight's intensity. As psychologist Carol Tavris cautions: "Expressing anger *while you feel* [*most*] *angry* nearly always makes you angrier."

I would go a step further. I believe that most of us can control the expression of anger for far longer than a few minutes or even hours. Here's another situation: Suppose you were told that if you cut back on screaming at your spouse (or children, friends, or employees) by 75 percent during an entire year, you would be given two million dollars. Do you think you would find a way to control your temper?

Obviously, we have more control over our rage than we are willing to acknowledge. For some, the control might be almost total; for others it might be far less. People who have less control must recognize the *moral* obligation to curb their harsh words. If they find themselves incapable of doing so on their own, they are *morally* obligated to seek the sort of professional help that will enable them to exert greater self-control.

Each year, large numbers of once-loving relationships, worth far more than two million dollars, are destroyed because of the hateful things people say when angry. To counter this, we must destroy the myth that Michal and David, and you and I, cannot control what we say or do.

Dr. Stephen Marmer, a psychiatrist, recommends that in dealing with anger we should think in terms of layers, or cascades, of control:

1. Control of our initial reaction

2. Control of our initial response

3. Control of our initial reaction to the other's response

4. Control of our succeeding reactions

Moving down this list, the degree of control grows progressively greater. Thus, even if you have not controlled your initial response, you can exert greater control over your next response, and work to repair any damage you might have caused earlier. Indeed, one of the saddest things about the David–Michal story is that the Bible records no effort by either to repair the damage caused by their tactless and cruel words.

This is not to say that it is wrong to feel anger or to express it, *within ethical limits.* When Maimonides, perhaps the greatest Jewish philosopher, wrote on the need to control one's temper, he also warned that a person should not become so indifferent to what others do that he becomes like a corpse, totally incapable of feeling.[5] Maimonides's cautionary words might well have been in response to the extreme strictures expressed by some Roman thinkers against ever expressing anger. Seneca, the first-century Stoic philosopher, argued that people could control their tempers no matter what the provocation. He cited the story of Harpagus, who, instead of going into a rage when a

Persian king presented him with the heads and flesh of his own children, responded bloodlessly: "At the king's board, any kind of food is delightful."*

What Maimonides proposes instead is an emotional golden mean: "[A person] should . . . display anger only when the matter is serious enough to warrant it, in order to prevent the matter from recurring."[6] In this regard he might well have been influenced by the nuanced advice of Aristotle, of whom Maimonides was a lifelong student: "It is a slavish nature that will submit to being insulted or let friends be insulted unresistingly. . . . A person is praised who is angry for the right reasons, with the right people, and also in the right way, at the right time, and for the right length of time."[7] In other words, there is nothing wrong with feeling anger, and with expressing it, within certain prescribed and ethical limits.

If you've ever ruptured a close relationship with angry words, consider whether observing the following rule could have led to a different outcome: *Limit the expression of your anger to the incident that provoked it.* Focusing the discussion in this way enables the criticized party to feel that his or her whole being isn't being attacked. It was this principle that David violated in his cruel counterattack after Michal mocked his dancing. He could have responded in many different ways: "It hurts me that you attack me on this

---

*Some modern scholars note that Seneca wasn't really advocating such total passivity. Professor Solomon Schimmel, who discusses this passage in *The Seven Deadly Sins,* pages 88ff., argues that the reason for Harpagus's response was not indifference to his children's deaths: He feared, rather, being invited to eat more of his children's flesh. According to Schimmel, "Seneca only wants to demonstrate that we have the capacity to conceal even intense anger. Actually, he felt that a more honorable response for Harpagus . . . would have been to commit suicide rather than flatter monstrous kings" (page 252, note 7). The citation from Seneca himself is found in his chapter "On Anger," sections 291–293.

incredible day. I was overcome with joy, and I didn't control my dancing because I didn't want to"; or "I wish you'd give up your aristocratic ideas of how a king must act, and realize how wrong you are. I made myself more, not less, beloved in the eyes of the people by showing them that I am a creature of flesh and blood just like them." He could even have spoken more sharply: "You are the one who acted wrongly, Michal, by remaining in the palace, and acting coldly and indifferently on so great a day."

However, what David did wrong was to attack Michal at her point of greatest vulnerability. "It was before the Lord Who chose me instead of your father and all his family [that I danced]." These words were calculated to humiliate and devastate his wife; they were the equivalent of responding to a slap in the face with a shot to the heart.

Unfortunately, many people act as David did. In Somerset Maugham's *Of Human Bondage,* the protagonist, Philip, has a clubfoot. One reason for Philip's generally low estimation of human nature is the realization "that when his fellows were angry with him, they never failed to taunt him with his deformity."

We all have "clubfeet." In Michal's case it was the pain of her father's rejection by God. For someone else, it could be a weight problem, or the lack of professional success, or an unhappy love life. To bring another person's vulnerability into an argument is wrong, not "maybe" wrong, not "sometimes" wrong. But absolutely wrong. If you ever become tempted to attack someone where he or she is most vulnerable, stop yourself from doing it, as surely as you would stop yourself from punching a friend at whom you were upset. The worst time possible to allude to painful areas in another person's life is during a fight. You are likely to be much harsher, and the other person far less receptive if he thinks your comments are part of an attack. If sore points must be discussed, do so when you are feeling love for the person, not animosity.

Had David and Michal abided by this rule, they could have fought about the issue that provoked their anger, but their dignity, and hence their relationship, could have remained intact.

The flip side of expressing disproportionate anger is not expressing it at all. Many of us, when injured, tend to withdraw from the person who has hurt us rather than address the issue. This withdrawal violates the biblical injunction: "Do not hate your brother in your heart" (Leviticus 19:17).

When we learned this law as yeshiva students, my classmates and I found it unintentionally amusing. "Does that mean," one boy challenged our teacher, "that it's all right to hate somebody as long as you tell them to their face?"

"More or less," the rabbi answered, to our surprise. "Of course, it would be better if you didn't hate somebody, but when you're angry at a person, you should confront him or her. Otherwise, your anger will fester and grow."

By way of example, the teacher cited the biblical story of two half brothers, Amnon and Absalom, who were sons of King David. In one of the Bible's unhappiest episodes, Amnon rapes and then abandons Absalom's sister Tamar (who is Amnon's half sister). Afterward, Absalom never confronts his brother: "And Absalom spoke to Amnon neither good nor evil for Absalom hated Amnon" (II Samuel, 13:22). Ultimately, after two years have passed, he arranges to have Amnon murdered.

Whether or not Amnon deserved to die is beside the point, the teacher told us. Rather, we should note the Bible's words: "And Absalom spoke to Amnon neither good nor evil for Absalom hated Amnon." The Rabbis deduced from this that a person who remains unnaturally silent when an expression of anger is called for might later explode in murderous rage.

Of course, most of us suffer much less grievous provocations and, rather than overreacting to them by killing someone, we nurse our injuries in silence, talk about them to people who cannot help, or inflict our anger on innocent people. As psychologist Carol Tavris has written: "If you are angry at Ludwig, all the discussions in the world with your best friend will not solve the problem. Unless the discussions result in your changing your perception of Ludwig ('Oh, I hadn't realized he didn't mean to insult me') it is likely to reinforce your own interpretations, with the result that *you rehearse your anger rather than ridding yourself of it*. If you displace your anger by punching pillows, conjuring up vengeful scenarios, telling nasty jokes or hitting your child, your anger will not be diminished nor will the displacement be cathartic. This is because the cause of your anger remains unchanged" (my emphasis).[8]

When you are angry, remember that there will always be time to break irrevocably with your antagonist. Sharing your anger with many people might prematurely cause such a break.

If you do speak about the matter with others, choose people who might calm you down and help you to see things in a broader, less bitter perspective. Avoid those who could provoke your rage ("He said *that* to you? That's disgusting! What are you going to do about it?"). But most important, try to speak to the person with whom you are angry.

Focusing on the object of the anger also underscores the importance of direct communication between antagonistic parties. A rabbi I know in Los Angeles received a letter from a congregant who was unhappy about a certain development in the synagogue. The rabbi knew that the policy that had offended his correspondent had been established well before his arrival as the synagogue's spiritual leader. He showed the letter to the synagogue's president, who told him that he would personally draft a response, and explain the policy to the unhappy congregant.

There the matter ended—or so the rabbi thought. Some time later, the synagogue again received a letter from the congregant who explained that, since the rabbi hadn't responded to his letter, he felt that he had no spiritual leader in the congregation and was resigning his membership. He also noted that, when the congregation engaged a new rabbi, he would be willing to rejoin. In addition to asking that his letter be shared with the whole board, he sent the rabbi a copy.

The rabbi described to me his reaction when he read the congregant's letter: "All sorts of angry thoughts ran through my mind. I felt like writing him, 'I am sorry that

I drove as kind a man as you to write such ugly things. Furthermore, your need to suggest that my dying, resigning or being fired would prompt your return to the synagogue was gratuitously nasty.' "

Of course, he wrote no such thing. Upset though he was, he wisely read the congregant's letter to a fellow rabbi. When he finished, his colleague offered a surprising response: "The way this man phrased his letter was definitely angering. But with all due respect, you are not fully in the right either. The letter was addressed to you and, seeing how upset he was, you should have responded, if only to tell him that he would be hearing from the president."

The rabbi swallowed hard and remained silent for a while. "You're right," he finally said to his colleague. "Well, if the right is not all on my side, then why am I feeling so annoyed at this man?"

He thought about this question a while longer, and finally realized that had the complainant written him a second time, telling him how upset he was not to have received a response to his letter, he would have felt terrible. He would have been horrified to realize that he had hurt someone deeply, and would immediately have called or written the man.

Instead, the congregant had never informed him of his hurt and anger. Rather, he had shared his angry feelings with the rabbi's employers, the synagogue's board of directors, hoping thereby to inflame other people against him and to bring about his dismissal.

Instead then of being able to think clearly about the possible legitimacy of the man's critique, the rabbi responded with fury.

The moral? Always address your grievances to their source. Much wisdom still inheres in William Blake's old quatrain:

I was angry with my friend
I told my wrath, my wrath did end.
I was angry with my foe:
I told it not, my wrath did grow.

7

Fighting Fair

One day, Resh Lakish, a young man who was a gladiator and a bandit, saw Rabbi Yochanan, the leading
scholar of his age, bathing in the Jordan. The young gladiator jumped in after him, and the two began to speak. Impressed with Resh Lakish's physical appearance and obvious
intelligence, Rabbi Yochanan said to him, "Strength like
yours should be devoted to Torah."

Resh Lakish countered by saying: "Looks like yours
should be devoted to women," for Rabbi Yochanan was
an unusually handsome man.

"If you will repent," Rabbi Yochanan answered, "I
will arrange for you to marry my sister. She is even better-
looking than I."

When Resh Lakish agreed, Rabbi Yochanan arranged
the marriage; he also became Resh Lakish's tutor. Within

a few years, the ex-gladiator and bandit became one of Israel's leading scholars.

Sometime later, an argument arose in Rabbi Yochanan's yeshiva. The dispute was of a highly technical nature, focusing on that point during production when different items become susceptible to ritual impurity. Rabbi Yochanan argued that metallic objects such as swords, knives, and daggers are considered fully formed—and therefore susceptible to ritual impurity—only at the moment a smith hardens them in a furnace.

Disagreeing, Resh Lakish contended that they can only be judged completed at the moment the smith dips them in cold water.

Annoyed at being publicly challenged, Rabbi Yochanan sarcastically responded: "A robber understands his trade."

Stung by Yochanan's allusion to his disreputable past, Resh Lakish countered: "What good, then, have you done me by influencing me to give up my life as a bandit? Among the gladiators I was called 'Master,' and here too, I am called 'Master.' "

"What good has been done you!" Yochanan thundered. "You have been brought under the wings of God."

Almost immediately thereafter, Resh Lakish became gravely ill. The Rabbis were convinced this was because he had offended Rabbi Yochanan. Resh Lakish's wife, who was Rabbi Yochanan's sister, pleaded with her brother to pray for her husband's recovery, but he refused. "If not for my husband's sake," she implored, "then pray for the sake of my children, that they not become orphans."

"I will take care of your children if your husband dies," Rabbi Yochanan responded.

"Then pray for my sake," his sister pleaded. "Pray that I not become a widow."

"I will support you if your husband dies," was all her brother would say.

A short time later, Resh Lakish did die, and Rabbi Yochanan fell into a deep depression. The Rabbis sent Elazar ben Pedat, the brightest young scholar they could find, to study with him, hoping that the youthful sage's sharp mind would divert Rabbi Yochanan from his grief.

Rabbi Elazar Ben Pedat sat before Rabbi Yochanan, and each time the older rabbi uttered an opinion, he would say, "I know another source which supports what you are saying."

Rabbi Yochanan finally said to him, "Do you suppose you are like Resh Lakish? Whenever I stated an opinion, Resh Lakish would raise twenty-four objections to what I said. . . . He forced me to justify every ruling I gave, so that in the end, the subject was fully clarified. But all you do is tell me that you know another source which supports what I am saying. Don't I know myself that what I have said is right?"

Rabbi Yochanan turned away from the young man, rent his garments, and staggered about weeping. "Where are you, son of Lakish?" he repeatedly cried out.

In the end he lost his reason. The Rabbis prayed that God take mercy on him, and soon thereafter he died.[1]

The quarrel between Rabbi Yochanan and Resh Lakish is surely one of the Talmud's saddest stories.[2] Two men who are best friends have a falling out, and one dies before they can make peace. The survivor is so inconsolable that the only peace that can assuage his pain is death. Perhaps the most poignant aspect of the story is that the dispute that yielded such tragedy was over a relatively minor matter.

This story's most important lesson applies to everyone: No matter how angry you become during an argument, remain focused on the issues at hand. *Never use damaging personal information to invalidate your adversary's contentions.* An inability to follow this simple rule is what transforms so many relatively moderate arguments into angry quarrels, often leading to ruptures between friends and close family members.

For many years, when lecturing, I have asked audiences: "In how many of your families are there relatives who no longer are on speaking terms?" Almost invariably, a little over half those present raise their hands.

When I ask people to describe the origins of these family feuds, they usually report quarrels that began over minor matters and then escalated. What caused this escalation? The very intimacy of the relationship provided the adversaries with destructive information that they could use against each other, and also ensured that their harsh words would have an impact.

This is a common pattern in quarrels that rip families apart and destroy friendships. In one family I know, the fight between a brother and a sister began over their father's obituary notice. The local newspaper had reported that the deceased was living in his oldest son's house at the time of his death. Although true, this announcement infuriated the daughter, with whom the father had resided for many years before moving into his son's house. She was irate that her brother had not made sure to have this fact included in the obituary.

Within days of the father's death, every act the brother had ever done and of which the sister had disapproved was raised, dissected, and condemned during increasingly acrimonious exchanges. I suspect that the brother was soon responding with some angry recollections and charges of his own. Although this fight occurred more than fifteen years ago, the siblings have had only the most superficial contact since. Of one thing I am certain: The aged father, whose obituary notice had set off this dispute, would have been brokenhearted.

"Hatred makes a straight line crooked," an ancient Hebrew proverb teaches. When people become angry, their reason becomes "bent." Suddenly, someone who is ordinarily quite kind and responsible, such as Rabbi Yochanan, can say terrible things. Because he did not have a compelling argument with which to defeat Resh Lakish, Rabbi Yochanan employed a highly personal one: How could anyone prefer Resh Lakish's reasoning to his, given that the former had been a gladiator and thief?

When Resh Lakish did not back off from his challenge and, indeed, counterattacked Yochanan for humiliating him, the latter grew even angrier. An hour before their dispute, had you asked Rabbi Yochanan to name his greatest disciple and closest friend, he undoubtedly would have answered, "Resh Lakish." Yet now, after exchanging a few harsh words, even the prospect of Resh Lakish's death doesn't soften his attitude. "I'll take care of your orphaned children," he assures his sister. "I'll support you if you become a widow."

How irrelevant those guarantees were! She hadn't come to her brother because she was worried about financial support for her family; rather, she wanted the two most important men in her life, her husband and her brother, to make peace. She must have been thinking: If Yochanan goes to visit my husband even now, perhaps he can still recover. But because Rabbi Yochanan would not "un-harden" his heart, both men were ultimately doomed.

Every year, tens of thousands of families are split asunder, and close friendships are broken, because contending parties refuse to fight fairly. In a dispute with someone, you have the right to state your case, express your opinion, explain why you think the other party is wrong, even make clear how passionately you feel about the subject at hand. *But these are the only rights you have.* You do not have a moral right to undercut your adversary's position by invalidating him or her personally. It is unethical to dredge up past information about the person—information with which you're most likely familiar because of your formerly close association—and use it against her.

Yet people do so routinely, then become furious when the other person breaks off contact or fights back with similar arguments. Words have consequences, and if you use them to hurt people, your victims will find ways to hurt you in return. This is what happened between Rabbi Yochanan and Resh Lakish. The way to avoid such bitterness in your life is to learn how to fight—ethically.

8

How to Criticize, and How to Accept Rebuke

Whoever can stop the members of his household from committing a sin, but does not, is held responsible for the sins of his household. If he can stop the people of his city from sinning, but does not, he is held responsible for the sins of the people of his city. If he can stop the whole world from sinning, and does not, he is held responsible for the sins of the whole world.

—Babylonian Talmud, *Shabbat* 54b

Be not angry that you cannot make others as you wish them to be since you cannot make yourself as you wish to be.

—Thomas à Kempis

The prophet Nathan provides a biblical model of how to reprove someone effectively. When he learns that King David has committed adultery with Bathsheba and has arranged for her husband to die in battle, the prophet realizes that he must confront the king. He does so in private, intent on moving David to recognize the great evil that he has committed.

Nathan comes before the king and tells him of a minor but disturbing injustice that has recently been brought to his attention:

> *There were two men in the same city, one rich and one poor. The rich man had very large flocks and herds, but the poor man had only one little ewe lamb that he had bought. He tended it and it grew up together with him and his children: it used to share his morsel of bread, drink from his cup, and nestle in his bosom; it was like a daughter to him. One day, a traveller came to the rich man, but he was loath to take anything from his own flocks or herds to prepare a meal for the guest who had come to him; so he took the poor man's lamb and prepared it for the man who had come to him.*
>
> *David flew into a rage against the man, and said to Nathan, "As the Lord lives, the man who did this deserves to die! . . ."*
>
> *And Nathan said to David, "That man is you!" (II Samuel 12:1–7)*

Nathan knew that he had the moral responsibility to confront King David about his very serious offenses, but he also recognized the necessity of presenting his reproof in a way that would be effective, and thereby force David to acknowledge his wrongdoing. Had he confronted David "directly," labeling him an adulterer and also a killer, the king would probably have reacted defensively, as most of us do when caught doing something wrong. He might well have come up with a long list of excuses, perhaps something like: "I didn't intend to commit adultery, I was just overcome with passion. When Bathsheba told me she was pregnant, the last thing in the world I wanted was to have Uriah killed. I summoned him from the battlefield, then urged him to go home and spend the night with his wife. That way, he would have assumed the baby was his. But he refused. I even ordered him to go home—twice—and both times he disobeyed me. So he left me no choice. Had I done nothing, then he would have come back later and found Bathsheba pregnant with a child not his, and would have harmed her. Besides, what if it became known that I had slept with one of my officers' wives while they were off fighting for me? It might have caused them to mutiny. I am the king of Israel; the country's entire destiny rests on my shoulders. For the country's survival, it was my duty to have Uriah killed."

Instead, by depersonalizing his critique, Nathan enabled the king to see the issue's moral simplicity: He had taken another man's wife, just as the rich man had stolen the lamb that the poor man loved. Once David had pronounced his verdict on the fictitious rich man, "The man who did this deserves to die!" and Nathan responded, "That man is you!" the king had no choice but to acknowledge that he deserved the same withering condemnation. David finally understood that all the tortured rationales in the world could not wipe away his act of adultery and Uriah's innocent blood.

Thus, because Nathan knew how to offer criticism, David learned how to repent.

Fortunately, few of us will ever have to rebuke another person for such monumental offenses. However, in our closest relationships, we often have reason, and even the obligation, to offer criticism, whether it is to express justified anger (see Chapter 6), to protect innocent people from being harmed, or to benefit some other person. Indeed, the Torah includes criticizing those who have done wrong among its 613 commandments: "Reprove your kinsman, but incur no guilt because of him" (Leviticus 19:17).

Some scholars interpret the commandment's last words, "but incur no guilt because of him," as obliging one to speak up lest one share in the responsibility for another's destructive behavior. For example, if a friend is drunk and about to drive a car, this verse obligates you to do everything possible to dissuade him from doing so. Even if you don't succeed in changing your friend's behavior, if you don't make a serious effort to stop him from driving while drunk, you share in the guilt for any injuries he may cause.

This commandment also enjoins us to offer rebuke in less extreme instances. Perhaps you have a friend who verbally attacks his spouse, or tries to "improve" his child's behavior in a manner that humiliates the young person. Speaking up in such a situation usually is quite uncomfortable, but remaining silent is grossly irresponsible and helps ensure that the harmful behavior continues.

There is a second interpretation of "incur no guilt because of him" that has been offered by several thinkers: Although you're permitted, and sometimes obligated, to reprove another, it is sinful to do so in a demeaning or humiliating way. If you criticize someone in order to stop her from committing a serious misdeed, running the risk of embarrassing her might not seem so terrible (although, even in this case, the humiliation she feels will make it less likely that your words will affect her behavior). On the other hand, if you're reproving someone about a less significant matter (for instance, a child who has irresponsibly broken something), you're never justified in shaming that person. In this case, trying to eliminate a minor wrong causes you to commit a major one. Instead, your goal should be to find a way of criticizing that will inflict the minimum of hurt while doing the maximum of good.

Consider the following story told by the late Isaac Asimov, the author and editor of some 470 books, and regarded by numerous admirers as one of America's premier intellects. Asimov himself was forthright about his high self-estimation: "I have always thought of myself as a remarkable fellow, even from childhood, and I have never wavered in that opinion."[1]

If ever there was a person whose ego might have been impervious to tactless criticism, it would seem to be Asimov. Yet in his posthumously published memoirs, he recounts an incident that he could never forget.

As a fifteen-year-old high school student, Asimov had enrolled in a writing class taught by a man named Max N. The teacher's first assignment was to have the students write an essay. When he asked for volunteers to read their efforts before the class, Asimov raised his hand. "I had read only about a quarter of it," he recalls in his memoirs, "when N. stopped me and used an opprobrious barnyard term to describe my writing. I had never heard a teacher use a 'dirty word' before and I was shocked. The class wasn't however. They laughed at me very uproariously and I took my seat in bitter shame. . . ."[2]

Although hurt and humiliated, Asimov conceded then, and in his memoirs, that N.'s negative assessment of his writing was correct. He had attempted an affected literary style; what emerged was "absolutely, terminally rotten." So he took the teacher's negative reaction to heart, and a few months later wrote a lighthearted piece that N. printed in the school's literary journal; it was the first significant piece of work by Asimov that was ever published.

But when he thanked N. for running the piece, the teacher wounded him again, saying he'd published it only because he needed a light piece to round out the issue, and every other submission had a serious tone.

Seventy when he wrote his memoirs, Asimov knew that he was terminally ill (he died two years later, in 1992). Yet anyone who reads this account realizes how fresh his pain was, even after fifty-five years. "I hate very few people," Asimov writes of Max N., "but I hate *him*." He confides a longstanding fantasy: "I wish I had a time machine and could go back to 1934 with some of my books and some of the articles that have been written about me and say to him, 'How do you like that, you rotten louse? You didn't know whom you had in your class. If you had treated me right, I could have recorded you as my discoverer, instead of branding you a rotten louse.' "[3]

If even as self-assured a person as Isaac Asimov can be so devastated by harsh criticism—he describes this episode as "the hardest blow my ego has ever received"[4]—consider how many less hardy souls we may have wounded through tactless and wounding words.

To avoid being needlessly cruel, before you speak ask yourself the following three questions:

First: *How do I feel about offering this criticism? Does it give me pleasure or pain?*

"Love unaccompanied by criticism is not love," an ancient Jewish text teaches.[5] Yet, criticism unaccompanied by love won't help the person being criticized. If you realize that part of you relishes speaking out, you probably shouldn't. The insincerity of your concern, your pleasure at seeing your victim's discomfort, and/or your desire to hurt someone at whom you might be angry will probably be apparent. As a result, your listener probably will react defensively, and be unlikely to change. Imagine yourself in the place of the person being criticized: If you sense that the speaker is enjoying his or her task, wouldn't that provoke anger and denial in you rather than self-examination?

If your motives are pure (you really wish you didn't have to offer the criticism, but feel morally obligated to do so), this will shine through in the encounter. It's likely that the listener won't see you as an adversary who wants to inflict hurt, but as a friend who wants to help, a perception that will enable him to maintain self-respect ("He's criticizing me because he likes me, and thinks that if I just correct this trait, everything will be all right").[6]

Before you criticize anyone, think about the advice commonly offered to medical students: "Your first obligation is to do no harm." Unless you're confident that both the content and tone of your words will help the listener to overcome a designated flaw rather than demoralize him or her, keep silent.

Second: *Does my criticism offer specific ways to change?* Because it's difficult to criticize someone in a manner that will induce change, Maimonides, the preeminent medieval Jewish philosopher and rabbinic scholar, offered very specific tactical advice: "He who rebukes another, whether for offenses against the rebuker himself or for sins against God, should administer the rebuke in private, speak to the offender gently and tenderly, and point out that he is only speaking for the wrongdoer's own good. . . ."[7]

Contrast Maimonides's counsel with the behavior of Asimov's writing teacher. Maimonides advises the person who is offering the criticism to do so in private; the first time N. criticized Asimov, it was in public. Maimonides advises that one should offer the criticism "gently and tenderly"; N. spoke brutally to Asimov, both publicly and privately. Maimonides advises one to point out that the criticism is offered only for the listener's good. Yet, when N. criticized Asimov he clearly wasn't doing so for Asimov's sake.[8]

Imagine how a writing teacher who had compassion for Asimov might have responded. Rather than dismissing the young student with a vulgar word, he would probably have kept him after class and shown him how artificial his writing style sounded. Even if the teacher felt the need to offer a public critique in order to teach the rest of the class, he could have done so without making the young student feel so abject a failure. Is it not obvious that a teacher who liked Asimov, or at least felt some sympathy for him, would have searched for a gentler way to offer his criticism, and included specific advice?[9] N. spoke harshly because he *wanted* his words to hurt; he was precisely the sort of person who should not offer criticism.

Finally: *Are my words nonthreatening and reassuring?*

It is told of the nineteenth-century Jewish moralist Rabbi Israel Salanter that when he offered criticisms during public lectures, he would announce: "Don't think that I am innocent of all the offenses I am enumerating. I too have committed some of them. All that I am doing, therefore, is speaking aloud to myself, and if anything you might overhear applies to you also, well and good."

Salanter's technique can be very effective in making criticism sound nonthreatening and encouraging. If you yourself have grappled with the trait you're criticizing, be sure to say so. If you're not guilty of the fault, you can cite your own struggles with comparable faults and the efforts you have made to overcome them. Acknowledging your weaknesses shows your listener that you are not setting yourself above him or her. And describing your attempts to change may offer the person the inspiration or some strategies to do the same.

If you want someone to be open to your criticism, avoid making blanket statements that demoralize him. Confine your remarks to specific incidents. Critics who use words such as "always" or "never" ("You *always* mess up everything you touch" or "You *never* care about anybody except yourself") in effect compel their listeners to react defensively. What person, the critic included, would be willing to acknowledge that she "always messes up everything," or "never cares about anybody except herself"? And when directed against a child, words such as "always" and "never" can permanently distort the child's self-image.

Aside from being psychologically damaging, extreme accusations are unethical because they are almost always untrue. You yourself know that your listener does not *always* mess up everything.

We tend to use unconditional words when we are angry, a time when almost everyone exaggerates and otherwise distorts the truth. If you find that you do so often, recall these wise words of Simcha Zissel Ziv, a nineteenth-century Eastern European rabbinic sage; his advice, offered in the context of a classroom setting, has far broader applicability: "Very often a teacher will become angry at a student who is rebuked three or four times and still does not listen. Before losing patience, the teacher should ask himself if he always corrects his own shortcomings by the third or fourth reminder."[10]

Sometimes criticism is most eloquent when not expressed in words. Take the nineteenth-century Hasidic rabbi Israel of Vishnitz, who wished to affect the behavior of a certain banker. He was well aware that a frontal critique, even if accompanied by words of affection, almost certainly would backfire. Guided by the talmudic admonition "Just as one is commanded to say that which will be heeded, so is one commanded *not* to say that which will *not* be heeded,"[11] the rabbi used a different approach:

"Rabbi Israel of Vishnitz was in the habit of strolling with his *gabbai* [assistant] for a half hour every evening. On one such occasion, they stopped in front of the house of a certain wealthy bank manager. The man was known to be a *maskil,* a follower of the 'Enlightenment' movement, i.e., anything but a follower of the rebbe [the Hasidic term for a rabbinic leader]. Rabbi Israel knocked on the door and, when a servant opened it, entered the house. The puzzled *gabbai,* without asking a word, followed the rebbe inside.

"The bank manager received his distinguished guest respectfully and politely. The rebbe took the seat that was offered him, and sat for quite some time without saying a word. Knowing that protocol would deem it impertinent to ask the rebbe directly the reason for his visit, the host whispered his question to the rebbe's assistant, but the *gabbai* simply shrugged his shoulders. After a good while, the rebbe rose to leave, and bid his host farewell. The bank manager accompanied him to the door and, his understandable curiosity getting the better of him, asked: 'Could you please explain to me, rebbe, why you honored me with a visit?'

" 'I went to your house in order to fulfill a *mitzvah* [religious commandment],' the rebbe replied, 'and thank God I was able to fulfill it.'

" 'And which *mitzvah* was that?' asked the confused bank manager.

" 'Our Sages teach that "Just as one is commanded to say that which will be listened to, so is one commanded not to say that which will not be listened to." Now if I remain in my house and you remain in yours, what kind of *mitzvah* is it that I refrain from telling you "that which will not be listened to"? In order to fulfill the *mitzvah* properly, one obviously has to go to the house of the person who will not listen, and *there* refrain from speaking to him. And that is exactly what I did.'

" 'Perhaps, rebbe,' said the bank manager, 'you would be so good as to tell me what this thing is. Who knows, perhaps I *will* listen?'

" 'I am afraid you won't,' said the rebbe.

"The longer the rebbe refused, the greater grew the curiosity of the other to know the secret: he continued to press the rebbe to reveal 'that which would not be listened to.'

" 'Very well,' said the rebbe finally. 'A certain penniless widow owes your bank quite a sum for the mortgage of her house. Within a few days, your bank is going to dispose of her house by public sale, and she will be out on the street. I had wanted to ask you to overlook her debt, but didn't, because of the *mitzvah* of "not saying . . ."

" 'But what do you expect me to do?' asked the bank manager in amazement. 'Surely you realize that the debt is not owed to me personally, but to the bank, and I am only its manager, and not its owner, and the debt runs into several hundreds, and if . . .'

" 'It's exactly as I said all along,' the rebbe interrupted, 'that you would not want to hear.'

"With that he ended the conversation and walked away.

"The bank manager went into his house, but the rebbe's words found their way into his heart and gave him no rest until he paid the widow's debt out of his own pocket."[12]

Knowing how to offer criticism and effect change even when one is not directly criticizing—*that* is a trait we should all strive to acquire.

As challenging as it is to criticize properly, it is even harder to accept rebuke. When criticized, many of us deny or minimize the faults being pointed out; we blame somebody else, perhaps even the critic, or insist, both to the person offering the criticism and ourselves, that we cannot change. Even as the critic speaks, we are already formulating a counterattack.

According to the Bible, this problem is as old as humankind. When God rebukes Adam for eating from the tree of "the knowledge of good and evil," an act which God had specifically forbidden, Adam blames Eve. "The woman You put at my side—she gave me of the tree and I ate" (Genesis 3:12). In fact, the implication of Adam's words is that not just Eve but God too is responsible, since it was He Who put her at Adam's side. When God confronts Eve over the sin, she blames the snake. "The serpent duped me, and I ate" (Genesis 3:13). Note that Eve skirts the fact that she then encouraged Adam to do so as well.

Some years later, when God calls out to Cain immediately after he murdered his brother, "Where is your brother Abel?" the killer responds, "I do not know. Am I my brother's keeper?" (Genesis 4:9).

It would appear that the passing of centuries did not encourage people to be more open to criticism. The second-century talmudic scholar Rabbi Tarfon lamented: "I wonder if there is anyone in this generation who knows how to accept criticism, for if one says to another, 'Remove the chip of wood from between your eyes,' the other answers, 'Remove the beam from between *your* eyes.' "[13]

Of course, there are some cases when attacking—or, better yet, ignoring—the messenger is appropriate. If someone is constantly criticizing you for things you are doing wrong, and rarely tells you when you've done something right, there's a good chance the person doesn't like you and/or that these criticisms are overstated and unfair. In addition, the critic who makes you feel that your problem is immense and uncorrectable is not offering constructive advice. To criticize a person for an uncorrectable fault makes as much sense as a woman saying to a man, "I could really love you—if you were only an inch and a half taller." Such needlessly hurtful words serve no one's interests.

Most of us, if we are honest about it, can tell the difference between unproductive rebukes and well-intentioned ones. Yet even loving criticism—perhaps *especially* when it is loving, for it is most inclined to highlight our true faults—can be a bitter pill.

Many people, when criticized, fight back by saying, "So you think I have a bad temper? At least it hasn't alienated my children from me the way yours are alienated from you" or "You think I treated you unfairly in that deal? Well, it so happens that my reputation for honesty is higher than yours. If you think I am exaggerating, maybe we should ask some other people what they think."

Whenever you're tempted to employ so sweet an argument, keep in mind that even if your critic possesses the flaws of which you accuse him, *so what?* If what he says about you is true, the fact that he himself has *numerous* flaws is irrelevant.

A friend of mine hosts a radio talk show. Although he passionately espouses often controversial political views, he makes it a point never to insult callers who dispute his positions. Rather, he listens carefully to what they say, and always responds courteously. He told me that he reads every letter from his listeners, *particularly* those written by people who clearly abhor his views. "I am anxious to read what they say," he explained to me. "Maybe I did say something unfair or wrong. The fact that I might disagree with these people on so many other issues doesn't mean that every criticism they make of me is wrong."

If my friend sounds unusually open to others' criticism,

that is an acquired trait. In his early days as a public speaker, he often fended off his critics with sarcasm, biting wit, and occasional anger. He now says, "A person can't grow that way. You grow by hearing what your critics are saying, and learning to distinguish what's true from what's false. You certainly don't grow if you only listen to people who just offer you praise."

Even more than being commendable, my friend's attitude offers a good lesson. Of course, there's a good chance that the person criticizing us has numerous faults; indeed, she even might be guilty of the very flaw that she is pointing out in you. But unless we have reason to believe that her real goal is to undermine our sense of self-worth, we should quash such thoughts as *What gives her the right to criticize me? Look at her flaws.* Instead, we should ask: *"Is what she is saying true?"* Even if the critic's point is exaggerated, that is no excuse to reject everything she has said. Instead, we should ask: *"Is there some validity in the criticism? Can I take what she has said, and use it to improve myself?"**

Only someone who is already perfect doesn't need to learn how to accept criticism, but such a person does not exist.

---

*For people blessed with relatively thick skins, learning to accept criticism might not be difficult (I'm speaking of those who actually take seriously what their critics say, not those who shrug off and ignore all critical comments). For people who are more sensitive, it can be very difficult to listen carefully to critical words and not respond with anger or depression. According to Jewish tradition, if a person is known to reject all criticism, or to respond to it with great anger, you're under no obligation to proffer it.

If you are the kind of sensitive person to whom this applies, you might regard this ruling as a dispensation. However, it's hardly desirable. Having people conclude that you can't change any bad traits, and that it's a waste of time to try to help you do so, is hardly a great honor.

If it's difficult to accept criticism, try this experiment: The next few times you are being criticized, consciously try to change only one thing—your attitude toward the critic. Instead of reacting as if he or she were your adversary, remember this two-century-old challenge offered by the great Hasidic rebbe Nachman of Bratslav: "If you are not going to be any better tomorrow than you were today, then what need have you for tomorrow?"

Indeed, what purpose is there to life if you can no longer grow, change and improve? Animals live cyclically; for them, each day, as far as we know, is the same as the preceding one, at least in terms of the animal's personality traits. But human beings can grow, both through self-analysis and self-criticism, and through the insights and criticisms of others.

Criticism, with its underlying assumption that we are still capable of change, should stimulate us; it implies that our souls, not just our bodies, still are alive. Thus, we should regard someone who points out "mendable" faults with the gratitude we feel toward a doctor who diagnoses an ailment. This very comparison occurred to one of Rabbi Salanter's disciples, the previously mentioned Rabbi Simcha Zissel Ziv: "A person is willing to pay a doctor for trying to heal him; should he be any less grateful to one who helps him correct his spiritual failings?"

Rabbi Salanter used to speak of an insight that occurred to him while spending an evening in the home of a shoemaker. Late at night, the man was feverishly working by the light of a candle whose flame was near extinction. "Why are you still working?" Rabbi Salanter asked him. "Look how late it is; your candle is about to go out."

"It is late," the shoemaker agreed. "But as long as the candle is burning, it is still possible to mend."[14]

We can all use mending, and so should cherish those who can help us see how we might "fix" ourselves. Rather than reject them and their words, we should keep these candles burning.

9

Between Parents and Children

About two thousand years ago, a certain Rabbi Elazar was taking a leisurely ride alongside a lake on a donkey, and feeling very proud of his considerable scholarly achievements.

Suddenly, the Talmud informs us, "he chanced upon an exceedingly ugly man, who greeted him, 'Peace be upon you, my master.' "

The man's disagreeable appearance shattered the rabbi's good cheer; instead of returning the greeting, he responded: " 'You worthless creature! How ugly you are! Are all the people of your city as ugly as you?'

"The man replied: 'What can I do about it? Go tell the Craftsman Who made me, "How ugly is the vessel You have made." ' "

"Rabbi Elazar [immediately] realized that he had done wrong. He got down from the donkey and, prostrating himself before the man, said to him: 'I apologize to you; please forgive me!'

"The man replied: 'I will not forgive you until you go to the Craftsman Who made me and tell Him: "How ugly is the vessel You have made." ' "[1]

When I first came across this tale as a young rabbinical student twenty-five years ago, I was sure that it had never happened, but was a fiction created by the Rabbis to teach a moral lesson. How could anyone, never mind an esteemed rabbi, be so cruel as to mock another person's ugliness? True, the Talmud depicts Rabbi Elazar as repenting, but how could he have said such a thing in the first place?

Since then, I have learned more from life than from books. The notion that, in a moment of self-satisfaction, a man of great stature could say something vicious no longer shocks me. In the intervening years, I have heard stories from friends and acquaintances, and read memoirs of those who suffered equally cruel insults, *not from strangers,* but from parents, the very people who claimed to love them more than anyone else.

Unquestionably, children's behavior can be frustrating and sometimes enraging. It is easy for an overworked, anxiety-ridden parent to focus on a child's inconsiderate, disobedient, or disrespectful actions. If we find ourselves doing this, in addition to inflicting emotional harm on our child, we also are violating the important ethical norm of *ha-karat ha-tov,* "recognition of the good [another has done you]." For while the tantrums and self-absorption of young children truly can infuriate or unnerve us, it is not reasonable to judge them by adult behavioral standards. We should also realize that acts of disobedience rarely tell the whole story. As one child psychologist wisely advises: "Remind yourself that your child performs thousands of acts of self-discipline . . . which you do not notice. There are thousands of times when he did come when you called, did eat the food he may not have wanted because you wanted him to, did give up some pleasurable activity to do your bidding even though it was painful for him at the time, did not bother you when you were busy, and did not fight or argue with you or his siblings."[2]

"Of course," we think. How many parents have ever looked into the face of a child asleep in a crib or bed, and wanted to do anything but help, protect, and cherish him or her? Yet, no honest parent can say that he or she has never had an outburst of unchecked anger or never made a demeaning or insensitive remark to a child. What's more, most of us carry at least a few scars inflicted by the words of our parents:

—A woman, highly self-conscious about being flat-chested throughout her teen years, still quails at the memory of her father's teasing: "When are you going to grow breasts and be a real woman?"

—An accomplished lawyer, who as a young boy used to create minor disturbances in school, still chafes at his father's unkind threat: "Don't assume that we love you. In this household, you have to earn our love."

—Eleanor Roosevelt never forgot how her mother would speak lovingly to her younger brothers, but not to her. "If a visitor was there," the First Lady confided to friends, "she might turn and say, 'She is such a funny child, so old-fashioned, we always call her Granny.' I wanted to sink through the floor in shame. . . ."[3]

—A woman I know recalls being told by her mother: "Don't smile or laugh when you're in public. Your buckteeth are ugly, and you look terrible." To this day, whenever she laughs—and you can be sure that she almost always tries to suppress the impulse—this woman still covers her mouth with her hand.

Some of these examples of hurtful words said by parents may sound extreme, but it's not hard to recognize the tremendous power they have to wreak psychological damage. The enormous attention focused in recent years on the physical and sexual abuse of children is deserved, but fortunately children who suffer such abuse are still a distinct minority. However, the victims of verbal abuse are far more numerous. Yet, because this form of parental cruelty is rarely viewed as a serious matter, it's seldom discussed. This is unfortunate, since the victims often carry its scars to their graves.

I am not suggesting that parents must speak only kind and supportive words to their children, even when they act badly. They definitely have an obligation to teach their children right from wrong, and to criticize them when they misbehave. In Hebrew the word for parent (*horeh*) comes from the same root as that for teacher (*moreh*), an etymological suggestion that the parents' primary role is to teach. Indeed, parents who don't know *how* to teach and *when* to criticize run the risk of raising moral monsters.

The Book of Samuel tells us the story of Adonijah, son of King David, who, during the last year of his father's life, went around Jerusalem boasting that soon he would be king. What was the root of his callous arrogance and disrespect toward his still living and reigning father? According to the Bible, David bore some of the blame because, throughout his son's life, "his father had never scolded him [and said], 'Why did you do that?' " (I Kings 1:5–6).

The biblical choice of words here is significant. The text doesn't say that David's error lay in not denouncing Adonijah for his poor character and selfish nature. So all-encompassing an attack probably would have been demoralizing and thus counterproductive. Rather, David's error, the Bible suggests, was in not criticizing Adonijah's bad acts as they occurred, in never asking him, "Why did you do that?"

A European scholar, Johann Paul Friedrich, wrote two centuries ago: "If a child tells a lie, tell him that he has told a lie, but don't call him a liar. If you define him as a liar, you break down his confidence in his own character." By restricting criticism to a specific bad act, a parent is unlikely to damage a child's self-image.

Admittedly, finding the golden mean between being critical but not *overly* uncritical is difficult, but the alternative choice of many parents—vacillating between broad and destructive deprecatory comments, and tolerating behavior that shouldn't be tolerated—is far worse.

Several years ago, close friends found that they were constantly criticizing their ten-year-old daughter:

—her clothes were perpetually strewn around her room;

—she grabbed food with her hands straight off the plate, and seldom used her fork;

—she demanded things without saying "please" or responding "thank you" when she received them;

—she didn't look at people when they spoke to her; and

—she constantly broke into her parents' conversations, even when they were on the phone.

One night, her father realized that from the time his daughter came home from school until she fell asleep, he and his wife had subjected her to one long litany of complaints. He thought about how he would have felt had every aspect of his work and personality been criticized this way by his employer. Would his behavior really have improved or would he have lost all faith in his own competence? Would he have believed that his boss's constant rebukes were motivated by a loving desire for him to improve himself? Or would he have concluded that his boss probably didn't like him very much, and had a low opinion of his capabilities?

The following day, the couple decided that instead of trying to turn their daughter into a perfect ten-year-old, they would focus their efforts for the time being, on the one area about which they cared most: the child's moral character. From then on, politeness and gratitude, saying "please" and "thank you," became their one nonnegotiable demand of her. They realized that unless their daughter's behavior improved in that area, she would grow up to be an unpleasant, unkind, and ultimately intolerable person. However, if she ended up "a bit of a slob," that would be unfortunate but better that than feeling rejected by her own parents.

Through their behavioral transformation, the parents demonstrated that they had internalized Henry Wadsworth Longfellow's penetrating insight: "A torn jacket is soon mended, but hard words bruise the heart of a child."

Parents commonly err not only in criticizing harshly, but also in forgetting to praise (this applies, by the way, even if your children are well into middle age). In *Signs of the Times,* the religious writer Gottfried von Kronenberger relates an incident about a young mother who confessed to her pastor: "My little boy often misbehaves, and I have to scold him. But one day he had been especially good. That night, after I tucked him in bed and started downstairs, I heard him crying. I found his head buried in the pillow. Between sobs he asked, 'Mommy, haven't I been a pretty good boy today?'

"That question went through me like a knife," the mother told her pastor. "I had been quick to correct him when wrong, but when he had behaved, I hadn't noticed. I had put him to bed without a word of praise."

This common parental formula of "heavy on the criticism and light on the praise" causes children to go through life feeling inadequate as human beings and unworthy of being loved. Psychologist Haim Ginott advises mothers and fathers: "If you want your children to improve, let them overhear the nice things you say about them to others."*

Another way in which many parents verbally wound their children is through comparisons:

"Your brother never spills things. He tries to be careful. Why don't you?"

"Your sister always says 'please,' and 'thank you.' I wish you would be polite and considerate like her."

"Your brother and sister don't get into trouble in school. You're the only one who's always causing us aggravation."

---

*This advice applies to everyone, not just parents. I once came across the autobiographical reminiscences of a great pianist who remembered one day as a child, he was going up the stairs and overheard his piano teacher tell his mother, "The boy has golden hands." From that day, the pianist recalled, he regarded his own hands with a certain awe. No matter how difficult a challenge he confronted at the keyboard, he was undaunted; after all, he had "golden hands."

These sorts of comparisons spring to the lips of many parents, yet I can think of a few more obvious violations of the Golden Rule. How many women would appreciate being told by their husbands, "Tom's wife, Mary, also has a full-time job, yet she doesn't go around complaining all the time how overworked she is"? And how many men would like to hear their bosses say, "If you could only learn to be more like Bill, and be more precise and innovative in your work"?

Throughout my childhood, until I went to college, I was a poor student. I tended to find schoolwork boring, and while I would read books about topics in which I was interested, I rarely did homework in those subjects in which I had no interest. My lackadaisical performance caused my parents considerable consternation. Two of my older cousins, who attended the same school as I, had graduated as valedictorians. My sister, also older than me, was very studious and ranked near the top of her class. On several occasions, our school's principal berated me (in front of the whole class no less): "What is the matter with you? You're a terrible student. I don't understand why you can't do even half as well as your cousins and sister." Needless to say, his words did not induce any improvement in my academic performance.

I remain, however, permanently grateful to my parents. Frustrated as they must have been by my mediocre school performance, and as often as they spoke to me about taking my schoolwork more seriously, I *never* recall them bringing my cousins and sister into the discussion. My parents intuitively understood that every criticism that can be directed toward a child can be made without reference to another sibling. I am also grateful to my grandfather, a rabbinical scholar of note, who one day said to my principal (and told me later that he had said it), "You must not say such things to Joseph. One day he will become an important man and do great things, and you will regret having spoken so unfairly to him."

Perhaps I haven't quite lived up to my grandfather's prophecy. Who could? But whatever I have achieved in life, I know, is due in large measure to the healing, supportive, and sometimes critical words of my parents and to my grandfather's absolute faith in me.

Comparisons with siblings also are detrimental for another reason. Whether intended or not, such comparisons imply a parental preference for the other sibling. I often ask my audiences how many of them grew up feeling that one or both of their parents preferred one child over another. Many hands go up, and whenever those who felt less loved start to speak, deep expressions of pain gush forth.

Parents have an obligation to ensure that all their children feel equally loved and appreciated (even if, in the privacy of their bedroom, they may express preferences for one child over another). When they do not convey a feeling of love and appreciation, the damage they inflict is often lifelong. For with what greater disadvantage can a child go out into the world than with the feeling that even her own mother and father don't really love her.

In addition, comparing children undermines family unity. Instead of making them feel that they are part of one united family ("one for all, and all for one"), children come to see themselves as competitors for a finite amount of parental love and approval. This type of competition rarely brings out the best in anyone, and increases the likelihood that such children will not be close to each other when they grow up. The Bible tells us that Jacob loved Joseph more than his other sons, and made no effort to disguise his favoritism. He even had a special and exceedingly beautiful coat of many colors woven for Joseph. This, and other acts of favoritism, helped inflame Jacob's other sons against Joseph, and eventually they sold him as a slave into Egypt, telling their father that a wild animal had killed him (Genesis 37). The Rabbis of the Talmud concluded from this episode that "a man should never single out one of his children for favorable treatment, for because of the two extra coins' worth of silk [which Jacob had woven into the special coat he gave Joseph] Joseph's brothers became jealous of him, and one thing led to another until our ancestors became slaves in Egypt."[4]

As regards the words children direct to parents, it is worth recalling that the Fifth of the Ten Commandments legislates: "*Honor* your father and mother." Although on three other occasions, the Hebrew Bible commands love (of God, of one's neighbor, and of the stranger; Deuteronomy 6:5; Leviticus 19:18 and 34), it does not command *love* of parents. In so intimate a relationship, it is hard to do so; either love is present or it isn't. What the Bible does demand is a measure of respect, one that can be expressed even during those painful periods when love might be lacking. It means that even when a child is furious at her parents, she doesn't cut them out of her life (except perhaps in rare instances of when a child suffers real physical or sexual abuse at a parent's hands), and when she expresses anger, she suppresses saying, "I hate you," or "I wish I had had decent parents, not you."

Many children grow up having been deeply hurt by their parents' words; by the time they become adolescents and adults, many have learned how to fight back—also with words. Usually, they are quite successful at hurting their parents in turn, although the greater their success, the more pain they usually cause themselves. In his *My Daddy Was a Pistol, and I'm a Son of a Gun,* the late Lewis Grizzard recalls going through his father's meager possessions at the hospital where he died. In the dead man's coat, Grizzard found a letter that he had evidently been carrying for a long time: "It was a letter from me. I had written it six months before. It was short, maybe a page, typewritten. Down at the end, I had given him some grief about straightening out his life. I told him I would have to think twice about inviting him to my house again if he didn't promise he wouldn't show up drinking. I'd just signed my name. I didn't say 'love' or anything. I had just signed my goddamned name like I was a real hardass. I still wonder why he carried such a letter around with him for so long. Maybe he kept it as a reminder to do better. I don't know. Maybe he kept it to remind himself his only son was turning on him. Whatever, I never forgave myself for that letter. I can't get it out of my head he died not knowing how much I loved him."[5]

Wise parents are guided by the Talmud's advice: "Who is wise? One who foresees the future consequences of his/her actions"[6]—and bears in mind the tremendous power words can hold over children's lives.

10

The Cost of Public Humiliation

S ome eighteen hundred years ago in Israel, Rabbi Judah the Prince, the leading scholar of his age, was delivering an important lecture when suddenly he found himself in a very aggravating circumstance: A member of the audience who had eaten a large amount of garlic was emitting such an unpleasant odor that the rabbi found it difficult to concentrate. Rabbi Judah abruptly stopped speaking and called out: "Whoever ate the garlic, leave!"

Almost immediately Rabbi Hiyya, a scholar only slightly less prominent than the speaker, rose from his seat and started toward the back. Many other listeners, mortified by Rabbi Hiyya's public embarrassment, followed him out, and the lecture was canceled.

The next morning, Rabbi Judah's son confronted Rabbi Hiyya, and criticized him for spoiling his father's lecture.

"God forbid that I would ever trouble your father," Rabbi Hiyya responded.

"How can you deny what you did?" the son answered. "Wasn't it you who stood up when my father demanded that the one who had eaten the garlic leave?"

"I stood up only to avoid the public humiliation of the person whose breath was bothering your father. Since I already have a certain status among the rabbis, I was willing to accept the embarrassment of being publicly singled out like that. Imagine, though, if the person who had eaten the garlic was a rabbi of lesser stature than me, or worse, a student. *That* person would have been deeply humiliated, and likely would have become an object of mockery."*

So far we have been examining the cost of harsh words spoken in anger or criticism. But what of the occasional cruelties to which we are all prone? In the preceding example, Rabbi Hiyya was concerned with more than just guarding the unfortunate garlic eater's dignity. He also wished to prevent Rabbi Judah from violating one of Judaism's most serious ethical offenses: humiliating a fellow human being.

"Whoever shames his neighbor in public," the Talmud teaches, "it is as if he shed his blood."[1] The analogy is deemed apt, because a shamed person's skin blanches as the blood drains from his face.

Abhorrence at the thought of publicly shaming others, however, does not seem to preoccupy a large number of contemporary journalists, prominent figures, and opinion makers, or, for that matter, ordinary citizens.

*The Babylonian Talmud, *Sanhedrin* 11a, recounts this incident. I have greatly expanded on Rabbi Hiyya's terse explanation for his behavior, putting into his mouth statements that are only suggested in the text and commentaries.

In 1959 a prominent businessman donated half a million dollars to a university in Saint Louis, Missouri. The *St. Louis Post-Dispatch* assigned reporters to write a feature about him. The reporters soon discovered that the man had served three prison terms, totaling almost ten years, for forgery, larceny, and issuing fraudulent checks. In the thirty-five years since he had left prison, his record had been spotless; in fact, the FBI had cleared him for defense-related work. More significantly, there was no reason to believe that any of his current money, including the half-million dollars he had donated to the university, had been earned illegally.

Nonetheless, the reporters headlined the article, which initially was supposed to be complimentary: [SO-AND-SO] . . . MAIN UNIVERSAL MATCH OWNER, IS EX-CONVICT. The man's wife and son, both of whom did not know of his earlier criminal record, denounced the piece as "vicious," to which Raymond L. Crowley, the paper's managing editor, responded: "I think the stories simply speak for themselves."[2]

The Talmud's moral standard differs markedly from Crowley's. "If a person is a penitent," it teaches, "it is forbidden to say to him, 'Remember your early deeds.' "[3] Needless to say, it's even more cruel to spread embarrassing reports about the person *to others* when his or her subsequent behavior has been exemplary.

The *St. Louis Post-Dispatch* article was harmful to far more people than just this man and his family; it sent a very demoralizing message to everyone who has tried to undo past misdeeds. It told them that no matter how hard they try, through hard work, charitable contributions, or anything that constitutes "doing good," they will forever be linked to the worst acts of their lives; they can never win back their good name. Wouldn't this alone make a person feel that there is little point in changing his ways?

The irony of the message communicated by the *St. Louis Post-Dispatch* "exposé" is profound. Years earlier, criminal courts had justifiably punished the man for doing evil. Now, the newspaper was punishing him for doing good.

This case is unusual. As a rule, reporters and newspapers rarely go out of their way to humiliate someone against whom they have no grudge. More commonly, journalists, like many of us, are apt to shame only those at whom they already are angry.

The desire to humiliate adversaries is particularly common in politics. When South Carolinian Tom Turnipseed ran for Congress in 1980, his Republican rival unearthed and publicized evidence that Turnipseed once had suffered an episode of depression for which he had received electric shock treatment. When Turnipseed responded with an anguished attack on his opponent's campaign ethics, Lee Atwater (who later became famous as the director of George Bush's 1988 presidential campaign, but was then directing the Republican campaign in South Carolina) responded that he had no intention of answering charges made by a person "hooked up to jumper cables."[4]

What a grotesque violation of privacy and the dictum against publicly humiliating another! Atwater put into the voters' heads a vicious, graphic image that potentially poisoned not only their perceptions of Turnipseed, but of everyone who has had electric shock therapy.

Is it any wonder that some ten years later, when Atwater himself was stricken with an inoperable brain tumor, and found himself attached to unpleasant hospital machinery, that he was moved to write Turnipseed a letter asking forgiveness?

In contemporary America, one of the most prestigious and highly paid professions, the law, commonly encourages its practitioners to humiliate those who oppose them in court. Particularly among criminal defense lawyers, *humiliating* an opposing witness is sometimes regarded as a singularly effective way to discredit testimony. Seymour Wishman, a successful and well-known criminal defense attorney, recalls a difficult defense he had to mount for a client accused of raping and sodomizing a nurse.

Although Wishman had no reason to assume the nurse had fabricated the allegation, he was ecstatic upon learning that the examining police physician had neglected to mention in his medical report whether there was any physical evidence that force had been used against the nurse. This omission freed him to pursue a particularly aggressive cross-examination of the woman, one filled with reputation-damaging and humiliating questions:

> *Wishman:* Isn't it a fact that after you met the defendant at a bar, you asked him if he wanted to have a good time?
>
> *Witness:* No! That's a lie!
>
> *Wishman:* Isn't it true that you took him and his three friends back to your apartment and had that good time?
>
> *Witness:* No!
>
> *Wishman:* And, after you had that good time, didn't you ask for money?

Witness: No such way!

Wishman: Isn't it a fact that the only reason you made a complaint was because you were furious for not getting paid?

Witness: No! No! That's a lie!

Wishman: You claim to have been raped and sodomized. As a nurse, you surely have an idea of the effect of such an assault on a woman's body. Are you aware, Mrs. Lewis, that the police doctors found no evidence of force or trauma?

Witness: I don't know what the doctors found.

After the trial ended, Wishman was proud when the presiding judge congratulated him for dealing with the woman "brilliantly." He felt considerably less proud half a year later when he accidentally encountered the nurse at her workplace. As soon as she recognized Wishman, she started screaming: "That's the son-of-a-bitch that did it to me!"[5]

Of course, she was referring not to the alleged rape and sodomy, but to the verbal "rape" to which the lawyer had subjected her. According to Wishman, this encounter left him shaken and feeling somewhat guilty.

What *is* amazing is the lawyer's surprise at his own reaction. Why shouldn't he have felt guilty? It's difficult to imagine a greater cruelty toward, and humiliation of, a woman than to suggest that she was a prostitute who had made a false allegation of rape because she hadn't been paid.

Atwater's and Wishman's very sincere regrets bring to mind a striking image in the epilogue to George Bernard Shaw's play *Saint Joan*. The scene is set some twenty-five years after Joan of Arc has been convicted of heresy and burned at the stake. When a group of people gather to discuss her impact on their lives, one man says that he feels fortunate to have been present at her execution, because having seen how dreadful it was to burn a person, he subsequently became much kinder. "Must then a Christ perish in torment in every age," another character asks, "for the sake of those who have no imagination?"[6]

Is it just some journalists, politicians, and lawyers who lack the empathy to understand how wrong it is to humiliate others? Apparently many of us share in this failing, because the shaming of individuals occurs thousands of times each day. The settings in which this emotional pain is inflicted may be less public, but the damage done can be just as devastating:

Take the case of Joanne, a woman I know in her mid-thirties, who is a middle manager at a large corporation. Her job ideally requires her to make public addresses and briefings, but for years her professional advancement has been stunted because of her inordinate fear of public speaking.

To Joanne and her many friends, her extreme nervousness has never made sense. Since she has considerable professional expertise, and is very articulate about her work in one-on-one settings, there exists no *logical* reason for her to freeze up every time she is called to make an address in public.

In desperation Joanne consulted a psychologist, who hypnotized her. After inducing a deep state of relaxation, the psychologist instructed her to focus on any recollections or associations involving discomfort around public speaking. Joanne began to regress, and was soon vividly reliving a series of episodes that had occurred when she was seven years old. At that time, her parents had recently moved from

Chile to Brazil. Although Joanne quickly acquired an adequate grasp of Portuguese, she still made many grammatical mistakes. Unfortunately, her second-grade teacher delighted in summoning Joanne to the blackboard at the front of the classroom and questioning her on material the class had been studying. On several occasions when she answered correctly but made grammatical mistakes, the teacher would ridicule her. After a few such episodes, Joanne chose not to answer at all. "Why do you stand there like a dummy?" the teacher would ask her. "Do you expect the answer to drop down to you from God in heaven?"

Twenty-five years later, this highly accomplished adult still finds herself paralyzed when called upon to speak in front of an audience. The schoolteacher's gratification of a sadistic impulse has left Joanne with a lifelong emotional scar. To this day, she continues to go to great (and, from a career standpoint, self-destructive) lengths to avoid situations where she again might be humiliated.

Roberta, another woman I know, recalls a recurring and humiliating trauma from her teenage years. As a young child, she had been her mother's favorite. But when she became an adolescent and gained twenty pounds, her mother's expressions of love turned to withering verbal attacks.

Once, when her aunt was visiting, Roberta brought some food to the kitchen table. As she walked away, her mother said to her aunt in a loud voice: "Do you see how big her ass is, how fat she's become? Doesn't it look disgusting?" The mother repeated this sentiment many times, always in the presence of others.

During her high school years, Roberta would wait until every other student had left the room when a class ended; she did not want people to see her from the rear. Although she's now over fifty, and her mother has long been dead, her miserable physical self-image remains perhaps the largest part of the legacy her mother bequeathed her.

WHEN YOU'VE HUMILIATED
ANOTHER PERSON

The great Jewish writer Rabbi Milton Steinberg once said, "When I was young, I admired clever people. Now that I am older, I admire kind people." Steinberg understood that it's a greater accomplishment to be kind than to be brilliant.

Harry Truman might not have been the greatest intellectual ever to occupy the office of president. But in addition to his penetrating common sense, Truman possessed kind instincts, epitomized by the extraordinary care he took not to humiliate others.

In 1962, some ten years after he left the White House, Truman lectured before a group of university students in Los Angeles. During the question-and-answer period, a student asked him: "What do you think of our local yokel?" referring to California Governor Pat Brown.

Mr. Truman bristled and told the boy he should be ashamed of himself for speaking of the governor in so disrespectful a manner. He continued scolding the boy a while longer; by the time he finished, the student was close to tears.

What marks this story off as different from every other account until now is what happened next: "When the question period was over," writes Merle Miller, author of an oral biography of the president, "Mr. Truman went to the boy and said that he hoped he would understand that what he had said had to do with the principle involved and that he meant nothing personal. The boy said that he did understand, and the two shook hands. Afterward Mr. Truman went to see the dean to ask him to send reports from time to time on the boy's progress in school. The dean said he would. . . . I asked Mr. Truman if he had ever heard from the boy himself, and he said, 'He's written me two or three times, and I've written him back. He's doing very well.' "*[7]

Compare Truman's behavior with that of Winston Churchill, arguably the greatest statesman of this century and a man of penetrating mind and wit. In an adulatory compilation of Churchill's greatest quotes and quips, James Hume writes of an incident during the 1930s in which a teenager annoyed and heckled Churchill during a speech. The second time the young man spoke up, Churchill replied: "I admire a manly man, and I rejoice in a womanly woman—but I cannot abide a boily boy. Come back in a few years when your cause is as free from spots as your complexion [will then be]."[8] The boy's arguments might well have deserved to be attacked, but if this story is true, why did Churchill have to mock the fact that he had pimples?†

*President Truman's concern about not inflicting gratuitous hurt is confirmed in an anecdote related by Tip O'Neill, the late speaker of the House: "I met [President Truman] with a group of us freshmen when I came to Congress in 1953, and the conversation turned to Mamie Eisenhower [wife of the newly elected Republican president]. Truman said that he had no use for Ike. 'But leave his family alone,' the President continued, his voice rising. 'If I ever hear that one of you attacked the wife or a family member of the President of the United States, I'll personally go into your district and campaign against you' " (Tip O'Neill with Gary Hymel, *All Politics Is Local* [New York: Times Books, 1994], p. 35).
†There is reason to suspect that as Churchill grew older, he became far more sensitive to the power of cruel words to hurt; see page 24.

While there is little question that the British leader was a greater statesman and intellectual than Truman, it was Truman who had the awareness and sensitivity to realize—not ten years later or even one year later but immediately—that the public scolding he had given the boy, *even if justified,* could subject him to ridicule and contempt. Imagine how different Joanne's life would have been if the teacher who had mocked her had realized right away the unfairness and evil of what she was doing, and desisted and apologized.

Other observers of Truman have noted that being attentive to others' feelings was very important to him. In 1964, when newsman Eric Sevareid interviewed him about his presidential experiences, Truman commented: "What you don't understand is the power of a President to hurt."

Sevareid was struck by this remark. "An American President has the power to build, to set fateful events in motion, to destroy an enemy civilization. . . . But the power of a President to hurt the feelings of another human being—this, I think, had scarcely occurred to me, and still less had it occurred to me that a President in office would have the time and need to be aware of this particular power among so many others. Mr. Truman went on to observe that a word, a harsh glance, a peremptory motion by a President of the United States, could so injure another man's pride that it would remain a scar on his emotional system all his life."[9]

If an American president, constantly besieged with personal, administrative, and political demands, can find the time to reflect on whether his words unintentionally shame another, doesn't it behoove all of us to do the same?

GUIDELINES FOR ENSURING
THAT WE DON'T HUMILIATE OTHERS

What was it about Harry Truman that caused him to be so conscious of the damage words can cause? It wasn't an exceedingly mild disposition, for the many Truman biographies indicate that he was an impassioned man who frequently lost his temper. But even when he expressed anger, what stopped him from humiliating others, or caused him immediately to set out to repair the damage if he feared he had done so, was his conscious internalization of the observation he made to Sevareid: "What you don't understand is the power of a President to hurt."

Change "the power of a President" to "the power of words," and you realize that we all have the ability to shame others.

If you reflect for a few moments, you'll realize how many people you can wound verbally (and perhaps already have): your spouse, parents, other relatives, friends, and/or people who work for you.

The first step in ensuring that we don't abuse this power is to be aware that we have it; otherwise, we'll feel no need to guard our tongues.

While it is important to recognize the power of words to hurt, such recognition alone is certainly not sufficient to stop us from using words destructively. No doubt many readers have nodded as they have read each episode in this chapter, mentally acknowledging the great evil of shaming others. However, unless you make such an acknowledgment *again and again,* you will probably forget it, particularly during moments of anger.

A popular British story tells of a very prominent politician who one night had imbibed too much liquor, and stumbled into a heavy-set female member of Parliament from the opposition party. Annoyed, the woman said to him, "You are drunk, and what's more, you are disgustingly drunk." To which the British parliamentarian responded: "And might I say, you are ugly, and what's more, disgustingly ugly. But tomorrow, I shall be sober."

If you, like the politician in question, have a quick temper and pride yourself on having a sharp wit, it is important that you *reflect again and again on the moral evil of shaming another person.*

For Lee Atwater it was only when he was lying on his deathbed that it became obvious to him how cruel it was to have mocked one of the most painful episodes in another man's life. I am sure that had Atwater been taught throughout his life *again and again,* as I believe all of us must be taught *again and again,* that humiliating another person is as evil as going up to someone in the street and punching him in the face, he wouldn't have done so in the first place.

Similarly, if my friend Roberta's mother, who jeered at her for being overweight, had reminded herself repeatedly how hurtful her words could be—so much so that, *forty years later,* her daughter still looks contemptuously at herself in the mirror—would she not have learned to curb her tongue? I suspect she would have, for Roberta is certain that her mother loved her, since she expressed many warm feelings toward her daughter on other occasions. Yet because Roberta's mother never learned to reflect on her potentially destructive power of words, she didn't feel the need to restrain her tongue when angry. She went through life like a reckless child playing with a loaded gun, and never understood that words are like bullets, and the damage they wreak often cannot be undone.

An ancient Jewish teaching observes: "It would be bet- ter for a person not to have been born at all than to experi- ence these seven things: the death of his children in his lifetime, economic dependence upon others, an unnatural death, forgetting his learning, suffering, slavery, and pub- licly shaming his fellow man."[10]

The first six items on this list represent some of the most horrific fates imaginable. Anyone who knows some- one who has buried a child realizes that no parent ever fully recovers from such pain. Similarly, the prospect of becoming totally dependent on others, or even worse be- coming another's slave, is horrifying. As for "forgetting his learning," we have all heard of people committing suicide after being diagnosed with Alzheimer's disease. Although most people won't take so drastic a step, I suspect most of us would prefer to die than to go through life with severe brain damage.

It's striking that the Rabbis included "and publicly shaming his fellow man" on the listing of terrible occur- rences. Note that they did not say "being *publicly shamed,*" but "*publicly shaming* his fellow man." To the Rabbis, be- coming the kind of malevolent human being who humili- ates others is as appalling a fate as losing a child—or one's mind.

Why? Every monotheistic faith believes that our mental capacities are God-given and that human beings were brought into this world to do good. If it's wrong to squan- der the gifts bestowed by God, how much worse it is to turn them to such an evil purpose as deliberately hurting another!

Finally, remember that *it is when you are most upset that you need to consider your words most carefully.* Admittedly, thinking about the consequences of what you say before you say it is particularly difficult at such a time. Rabbi Judah the Prince was so bothered by the smell of garlic that he didn't reflect on the shame his words might inflict on the person who had eaten it. Winston Churchill was so annoyed by the young man's irritating behavior that he only wished to find a "put-down" that would make others laugh at the boy's unappealing physical traits. But while Rabbi Judah and Churchill were justified in being annoyed at the provocative behavior directed toward them, the "punishment" inflicted by their sharp words far outweighed the victims' "crimes."

Jewish law asks us to take care not to humiliate others even in far-fetched cases: "If someone was hanged in a person's family, don't say to him, 'Hang up this fish for me,'" lest you trigger that distressful memory or remind others who are present of the shameful event.[11] If we are supposed to be morally vigilant even in such a remote case, how much more careful should we be not to publicly mock someone's bad breath, acne, or ugliness.

If you have humiliated another person, of course you should apologize to him or her. But the far more moral thing to do is to exercise restraint *before* you inflict shame, for the greatest remorse and the best will in the world never can erase your words. You can do everything possible to try to minimize their impact, but unfortunately, that is all you can do.

11

Is Lying Always Wrong?

A truth that's told with bad intent
Beats all the lies you can invent.
—William Blake, "Auguries of Innocence"

"What words should people call out as they dance in front of a bride?" With this question, the Talmud inaugurates a strange debate.

The School of Rabbi Hillel answers that wedding guests always should exclaim: "What a beautiful and gracious bride!" The School of Rabbi Shammai disagrees. "If she is lame or blind, are you going to say of her, 'What a beautiful and gracious bride'? Does not the Torah command, 'Stay far away from falsehood'?" (Exodus 23:7). They thus insist that no standard formula be recited; rather, each bride should be described "as she is."

"According to your words," the followers of Hillel respond,

"if a person has made a bad purchase in the market, should one praise it to him or deprecate it? Surely [you would agree that] one should praise it to him. Therefore, the Rabbis teach, 'One's disposition should always be pleasant with people.' "[1]

This talmudic debate highlights a question that religious and secular thinkers have been considering for millennia: When, if ever, is it appropriate to lie?

A surprising number of ethicists have answered, "Never." Not only would they not sanction the sort of tactful words advocated by Hillel, they feel it is wrong to lie even when life is at stake.

The fourth-century Saint Augustine, arguably the preeminent Church Father, is the most forceful Christian advocate of this position. He believed that, since telling an untruth costs a person eternal life, lying to save a life is foolish and unjustifiable: "Does he not speak most perversely who says that one person ought to die spiritually, so another may live? . . . Since then, eternal life is lost by lying, a lie may never be told for the preservation of the temporal life of another."[2]

Augustine's absolutist position influenced some very heroic Catholics to feel that they had behaved immorally because they lied. Father Rufino Niccacci, a peasant priest who saved three hundred Jews in Assisi from the Nazis by providing them forged identity papers and helping them blend into the non-Jewish community, was troubled by the deception in which he had participated: "I became a cheat and a liar, for a good cause, mind you, but nevertheless a sinner, although I am sure that I have long since made my peace with God, and that He has forgiven my trespass."[3] Apparently Father Niccacci regarded people who refused to tell such lies (and thus save innocent lives) as on some level less sinful than he.

For the eighteenth-century Immanuel Kant, perhaps the modern era's most influential philosopher, telling the truth was a universal moral absolute that allowed for no exceptions. In an essay, "On a Supposed Right to Tell Lies from Benevolent Motives," Kant contended that if a would-be murderer inquires whether "our friend who is pursued by him has taken refuge in our house," we are forbidden to lie and mislead him.*[4] Kant goes so far as to say that if you respond accurately to the would-be killer's question about the location of his intended victim, you incur no moral guilt for the ensuing murder. However, if you lie to the murderer, saying, for example, that your friend is no longer home, but unbeknownst to you he really *has* gone out, and "the murderer had then met him as he went away and murdered him, you might justly be accused of being the cause of his death. For if you had told the truth . . . perhaps the murderer might have been apprehended by the neighbors while he searched the house and thus the deed might have been prevented. Thus, whoever tells a lie, however well-intentioned he might be, must answer for the consequences, however unforeseeable they were, and pay the penalty for them even in a civil tribunal." (A reader of Kant's essay may feel that, emotionally, Kant seems to have almost as great an anger at the liar who tried to deceive the murderer as at the killer himself.)

The Hebrew Bible's view differs sharply from both Augustine's and Kant's. When life is at stake, the Bible depicts God as not only permitting lying, but even mandating it. For example, when God commands the prophet Samuel to

---

*In an analysis of *Lying*, philosopher Sissela Bok points out that according to Kant's ethics, a ship captain transporting refugees from Nazi Germany shouldn't have lied to the captain of a patrolling German vessel who asked whether there were Jews aboard.[5]

Bok's example is apt, for in no country did Kant exert a greater influence than in his native Germany. Yet a German who would have looked to him for moral guidance during the Nazis' murderous rule would have found himself forbidden to lie to Nazi officials in order to save innocent lives.

anoint David as king in place of Saul, Samuel refuses. "How can I go? If Saul hears about it, he will kill me" (I Samuel 16:2).

God neither promises Samuel protection nor tells him to speak truthfully and bear the consequences. Rather, He instructs the prophet to tell Saul a lie, that his trip's purpose is not to anoint a new monarch, but to offer a sacrifice. Apparently God wishes to teach Samuel that one does not owe the truth to would-be murderers.

What of the situation that most of us face—when lying will not preserve a life, but will spare feelings? Imagine Kant at a wedding, speaking to a groom:

"What do you think of my bride, Professor?"

"Well, it is clear from looking at her that you did not marry her for her beauty, and from speaking to her, I can see that she is not in possession of a powerful intellect. Then again, perhaps she is very kind. I cannot say that for a fact, of course, since I only spent a few minutes with her."

"Thank you for being so honest about your observations, Professor, but I want you to know that what you have said hurt me."

To which Kant might well have responded, with words drawn from his previously cited essay, "Truthfulness in statements . . . is the formal duty of an individual to everyone, however great may be the disadvantage accruing to himself or to another."

Such an "I don't care what the cost is" fidelity to truth creates a very inhospitable dynamic.

Concerning other verbal exchanges, Jewish teachings offer a wealth of advice on when and how to bend the truth, and when not to. As an example of when *not* to lie, the Talmud offers the somewhat humorous example of Rav, whose wife would torment him by cooking the opposite of what he requested. If he asked for lentils, she gave him peas; if peas, she gave him lentils.

When his son Hiyya became older and realized what his mother was doing, he would invert his father's requests to her. If Rav told him he wanted lentils, the boy would tell his mother that he had requested peas.

One day, Rav said to his son, "Your mother has improved." To which Hiyya responded: "That's because I inverted your messages."

Although appreciative of his son's cleverness, Rav instructed him not to do so anymore, because "it is evil to accustom one's tongue to speak lies."[6]

Rav was willing to forgo the convenience that accrued from his son's lies in order to ensure that the boy grew up to be truthful. The contemporary implication is that we too should not accustom a child to lie on our behalf, whether to unwanted phone callers ("Tell them Daddy isn't at home") or ticket agents at movie theaters ("Tell them you're only eleven"). A child raised by his parents to lie and cheat for their convenience will quickly learn to lie and cheat for his own convenience.

According to the Talmud, it also is very wrong for a parent to lie to a child. "One should not promise a child something, and then not give it to him, because as a result the child will learn to lie."[7] When a parent promises a gift to a child and does not "deliver," the child may at first be bitterly disappointed, but eventually will conclude cynically that this is how the real world works.

The Talmud further legislates that it is wrong to lie or mislead a person if your goal is to secure some personal advantage. For example, it is forbidden to invite someone to be your guest if you know that he or she will refuse, since your goal is to make the person feel indebted or grateful to you for something you never intended to do.[8] Likewise, it is not permitted to open an expensive bottle of wine and tell a guest that you are doing so in his honor, when it was your intention to uncork it in any event.[9] On the other hand, if the guest drew the wrong inference and said, "I am deeply touched that you served such wonderful wine in my honor," then the guest is misleading himself, a misapprehension that you are not obligated to correct, at the cost of causing him pain.

Indeed, where one's goal is to avoid inflicting gratuitous emotional pain on another, Jewish law becomes remarkably tolerant of half-truths and "white lies." For example, Genesis 18 records the visit of three angels to Abraham and Sarah, at a time when Abraham was ninety-nine years old and his wife, eighty-nine.

The angels tell Abraham that within the year Sarah will give birth. Listening nearby, Sarah laughs to herself, saying: "Now that I am withered, am I to have enjoyment, with my husband so old?"

In the next verse, God asks Abraham: "Why did Sarah laugh, saying, 'Shall I in truth bear a child, old as I am?'" (Genesis 18:12–13). Compare Sarah's words with God's, and you'll note that God doesn't transmit her entire comment to Abraham: He omits Sarah's reference to Abraham being "so old," presumably out of concern that such a comment might hurt or anger him. On the basis of this passage, the Talmud concludes: "Great is peace, seeing that for its sake even God modified the truth."[10]

According to rabbinic teachings, Aaron, Moses' older

brother and the High Priest, valued making peace between feuding parties so highly that he flat-out lied to achieve this end. In a well-known *midrash* (a rabbinic commentary on a biblical text), the Rabbis relate:

"When two men had quarreled, Aaron would go and sit with one of them and say, 'My son, see what your friend is doing! He beats his breast and tears his clothes and moans, "Woe is me! How can I lift my eyes and look my companion in the face? I am ashamed before him, since it is I who treated him foully." Aaron would sit with him until he had removed all anger [literally, jealousy] from his heart.

"Then, Aaron would go and sit with the other man, and say likewise, 'My son, see what your friend is doing! He beats his breast and tears his clothes and moans, "Woe is me! How can I lift my eyes and look my companion in the face? I am ashamed before him, since it was I who offended him." Aaron would sit with him also until he had removed all anger from his heart.

"Later, when the two met, they would embrace and kiss each other."[11]

The Rabbis endorse Aaron's behavior, not because Jewish law approves of lying per se—it does not—but because it recognizes that in cases where peace and truth conflict, peace should sometimes take precedence.[12]

As a general principle, lying can be considered moral when the truth can do no good but only cause pain. Thus, if a person about to go to a party puts on a dress or a suit that is unattractive, and asks how she or he looks, you should respond truthfully. By doing so, you will perhaps save the person from embarrassment. But if you meet someone at a party in those same garments, and the person asks the same question, it would be pointless, and gratuitously cruel, to answer: "You look terrible," even if it's what you think.

There are a few specific instances when Jewish tradition actively encourages lying. From Judaism's perspective, life is almost always a higher value than the truth, so that you certainly do not owe "just the facts" to a criminal who will use them to murder someone. (You're also entitled to lie to a thief concerning the whereabouts of an object he wishes to steal. In certain instances, particularly where you are dealing with an unscrupulous person, preserving property is also a higher value than truth.) As we discussed in Chapter 2, if an individual asks you what someone has said about her, you're permitted, indeed obligated, to leave out negative comments (except in certain rare cases; see page 31). If the person continues to press you for information—"What else did he say?"—you're permitted to lie if necessary and answer, "Nothing else. He said nothing negative." Jewish law places one restriction on this rare permission to lie: taking an oath to a false statement ("I swear in God's name that he only said wonderful things about you"). To swear to something untrue in the name of God is never allowed (except when an innocent life is at stake).*

Thus, from Judaism's perspective, truth is a very important value but not an absolute one.

While most lying is reprehensible (who wants to be friends with a person whose statements you can't trust?) people who pride themselves on *always* being truthful sometimes use this as an excuse to become verbal sadists. In his autobiographical *A Writer's Notebook,* Somerset Maugham conveys how a cruel truth, told solely to benefit the speaker,

*Indeed, such an act is specifically prohibited by the Ninth Commandment.

wrought an unbearable consequence. A woman who had become pregnant during an adulterous affair waited some thirty years to tell her husband that the son he so cherished was not his. Within days, the man committed suicide. Upon learning of his death, the wife, who was suffering from mental instability and had been told that her husband had died in an accident, said, "Thank God, I told him when I did. If I hadn't, I should never have had another moment's peace in my life."[13]

I would designate such a person as a malevolent truth teller. She didn't inform her husband of her adultery at the time it occurred, perhaps because she wanted to retain the advantages of living with him, as he was a wealthy man. Instead, she waited decades until her husband had forged a very close bond with the boy he assumed was his. Now that she was suffering from mental instability, and perhaps was incapable of enjoying *her* life, she wished to see her husband suffer as well. Telling the truth *at the time she chose to do so* was an even more evil act than her original act of adultery.

Verbal sadism is common and particularly harmful within marriages. For example, during a time of marital tension, a man I know told his wife about six different women he knew to whom he was more attracted than her, and how much he fantasized about sleeping with them. Likewise, parents who make it clear to their child that they prefer one of his or her siblings are guilty of such sadism.

Not surprisingly, in the talmudic debate that began this chapter, the tradition ends up ruling in favor of Hillel, who advocates praising the bride, in deference to her (and the groom's) feelings. As the hero of Graham Greene's novel *The Heart of the Matter* says: "In human relations, kindness and lies are worth a thousand [gratuitously painful] truths."[14]

"MACRO" LIES

Until now, we have focused on "micro" lies, untruths that are told to protect other people's feelings or safety. Essayist Dennis Prager makes the point that while ethical considerations allow some (though by no means all) such untruths, it is impermissible to lie about "macro" issues that transcend the individual.

"Macro" lies can be particularly pernicious. For example, *The Protocols of the Elders of Zion,* a late nineteenth-century forgery allegedly revealed an international Jewish conspiracy to take over the world and to plunge nations into warfare and poverty. Historian Norman Cohn has documented how the Nazis cited *The Protocols* as a "warrant for genocide" against the Jews. During the Holocaust, six million Jews, of whom over one million were children, were murdered; the *Protocols'* lies helped set the stage for their annihilation.[15]

In contrast to the preceding example, "macro" lies often are told by those who are motivated by a desire to mobilize large numbers of people on behalf of a noble cause. But the use of ignoble means to achieve noble ends often results in new forms of immorality. For example, impelled by the desire to rally public opinion against Germany during World War I, Allied propagandists concocted tales of terrible atrocities carried out by German occupation troops. Soldiers were accused of tossing infants into the air and impaling them on their bayonets, cutting off children's hands, and raping nuns. These stories were widely believed and endorsed by, among others, the noted historian Arnold Toynbee.[16] While such lies helped unite citizens of Allied countries and motivate their troops, they also stimulated anti-German hatred and occasionally provoked physical attacks against Americans of German descent.

When World War I ended, it became widely known that although German rule had been harsh, and deserved criticism, its soldiers had never carried out the atrocities of which the propagandists had accused them.

Adolf Hitler was among the few people who thought that telling "macro" lies was a good strategy. He wrote in his political autobiography *Mein Kampf:* "The British and American war propaganda was psychologically correct. By displaying the German to their own people as a barbarian and a Hun, they were preparing the individual soldier for the horrors of war, and . . . heightened his rage and hatred against the villainous enemy."[17]

More than twenty years later, during World War II, when stories again began to circulate of terrible atrocities committed by German troops, this time, they were all too true. But many people rejected the reports, citing the lies told during World War I. They argued that once again a similar kind of anti-German propaganda was being spread. Thus, an immoral lie told during World War I was a factor in discouraging people from believing true reports of Nazi atrocities. If more people had believed what Nazi victims were saying, greater efforts on their behalf might have been undertaken.

Undoubtedly, the creators and disseminators of World War I anti-German propaganda felt it was noble to lie in behalf of a worthwhile cause. They were wrong, and more than two decades later, tens of thousands of innocent victims may well have paid the price for their moral error.

People's tendency to tell untruths is perhaps most disturbing when they're espousing high-minded causes. For example, many feminists justifiably feel that American society has put great and unfair emphasis on women being thin, and regard the eating disorder anorexia nervosa as a perverse consequence of this. Unfortunately, in their desire to horrify listeners and readers about the disease's horrors, some leading feminist writers seem to have concluded that the truth needs to be "helped along."

In *Revolution from Within*, Gloria Steinem informs readers that "in this country alone . . . about 150,000 females die of anorexia each year."[18] Were this figure accurate, it would mean that more than one million American women die from this eating disorder during a seven-year period.

Steinem cites Naomi Wolf's best-selling *The Beauty Myth* as a source for her statistic. The number of alleged deaths from, and the sufferings of victims of, anorexia so shocked Wolf that she noted that although "nothing justifies comparison with the Holocaust . . . when confronted with a vast number of emaciated bodies starved not by nature *but by men,* one must notice a certain resemblance [my emphasis]."[19]

Wolf, in turn, cites as *her* source, *Fasting Girls: The Emergence of Anorexia Nervosa as a Modern Disease* by Joan Brumberg, a historian and the former director of women's studies at Cornell University. Brumberg posits that these 150,000 annual deaths are due to "a misogynistic society that demeans women . . . by objectifying their bodies."[20] Thus, it is allegedly men who are responsible for the deaths of tens of thousands of women. Brumberg attributes the statistic to the American Anorexia and Bulimia Association.

Philosophy professor Christina Hoff Sommers, author of *Who Stole Feminism?*, was puzzled by this statistic. If over a million women had died from anorexia in the preceding seven years, how was it possible that she didn't know many, let alone any? One wonders whether the same question hadn't occurred to Brumberg and the writers who cited her. As of 1994, fewer than 300,000 Americans have died from AIDS, yet obituaries of the disease's victims frequently appear in newspapers. Very rarely, if ever, does one read of a woman succumbing to anorexia (a rare exception was Karen Carpenter, lead singer of The Carpenters).

When Sommers contacted Dr. Diane Mickey, the American Anorexia and Bulimia Association's president, she learned that its carefully researched statistics had been seriously altered. In a 1985 newsletter, the association had written that 150,000 to 200,000 American women suffer from anorexia nervosa. This represented the sum total of American women *afflicted* with the disorder, not the number who die from it annually.

According to the National Center for Health Statistics, 101 women died from anorexia nervosa in 1983; 67 in 1988. The Division of Vital Statistics of the National Center for Health Statistics reported 54 deaths from anorexia in 1991 (none from bulimia), or *about 1/3000th of the number reported by Brumberg, and cited by Steinem and Wolf.* Concludes Professor Sommers: "The deaths of these young women are a tragedy, certainly, but in a country of one hundred million adult females, such numbers are hardly evidence of a 'holocaust.' "[21]

Unfortunately, once best-selling authors introduce such "facts" to millions of readers, their data, and the conclusions resulting from them, become widely accepted. In

April 1992, Ann Landers wrote in her syndicated advice column: "Every year, 150,000 American women die from complications associated with anorexia and bulimia." *The Knowledge Explosion,* a university textbook for women's studies courses, also contains this figure in its preface.

Apparently the goal in spreading highly exaggerated statistics—when one refers to distortion on a scale of 1,500- to 3,000-fold, the word "exaggeration" seems an understatement—is not only to alarm readers about a dreaded disease, but to provoke great anger at men. It is men, and the beauty standards they have supposedly conditioned women to strive for, that are responsible for the alleged deaths of 150,000 women annually.

In conclusion, "macro" lies are immoral. If you believe that telling such untruths is the only way you can buttress an argument, consider whether your cause is just and persuasive enough not to have to rely on distortions of the truth.

PART

FOUR

Words That Heal

Rabbi Beroka . . . used to frequent the marketplace in Be Lefet [a city in Persia] where Elijah often appeared to him. Once, Rabbi Beroka asked him, "Is there anyone in this marketplace who has a place in the World-to-Come?"

Elijah replied, "No . . ."

In the meantime, two men walked by. Elijah remarked, "These two have a share in the World-to-Come."

Rabbi Beroka asked them, "What is your occupation?"

They replied, "We are comedians. When we see people who are depressed, we cheer them up; also, when we see two people quarreling, we strive hard to make peace between them."

—Babylonian Talmud, Ta'anit 22a

12

Words That Heal

A rt Buchwald, the humorist who wrote the following
column, shows us the great good a single individual
can accomplish through a few simple words and deeds.

*I was in New York the other day and rode with a friend in
a taxi. When we got out, my friend said to the driver,
"Thank you for the ride. You did a superb job of driving."*

*The taxi driver was stunned for a second. Then he said,
"Are you a wise guy or something?"*

*"No, my dear man, and I'm not putting you on. I
admire the way you keep cool in heavy traffic."*

"Yeh," the driver said and drove off.

"What was that all about?" I asked.

*"I am trying to bring love back to New York," he said.
"I believe it's the only thing that can save the city."*

"How can one man save New York?"

"It's not one man. I believe I have made the taxi driver's day. Suppose he has twenty fares. He's going to be nice to those twenty fares because someone was nice to him. Those fares in turn will be kinder to their employees or shop-keepers or waiters or even their own families. Eventually the goodwill could spread to at least 1,000 people. Now that isn't bad, is it?"

"But you're depending on that taxi driver to pass your goodwill to others."

"I'm not depending on it," my friend said. "I'm aware that the system isn't foolproof, so I might deal with ten different people today. If, out of ten, I can make three happy, then eventually I can indirectly influence the attitudes of 3,000 more."

"It sounds good on paper," I admitted, "but I'm not sure it works in practice."

"Nothing is lost if it doesn't. It didn't take any of my time to tell that man that he was doing a good job. He neither received a larger tip nor a smaller tip. If it fell on deaf ears, so what? Tomorrow there will be another taxi driver whom I can try to make happy."

"You're some kind of a nut," I said.

"That shows how cynical you have become. . . ."

We were walking past a structure in the process of being built and passed five workmen eating their lunch. My friend stopped. "That's a magnificent job you men have done. It must be difficult and dangerous work." The five men eyed my friend suspiciously. "When will it be finished?"

"June," a man grunted.

"Ah, that really is impressive. You must all be very proud."

We walked away. I said to him, "I haven't seen anyone like you since 'The Man of La Mancha.' "

"When those men digest my words, they will feel better for it. Somehow the city will benefit from their happiness."

"But you can't do this alone," I protested. "You're just one man."

"The most important thing is not to get discouraged. Making people in the city become kind again is not an easy job, but if I can enlist other people in my campaign . . ."

"You just winked at a very plain looking woman," I said.

"Yes, I know," he replied. "And if she's a school-teacher, her class will be in for a fantastic day."[1]

Imagine what life would be like if Buchwald's friend did manage to enlist many others in his campaign.

Unfortunately, we are far from achieving such a utopian world. In fact, many of us are too caught up in our own problems, or too lazy, indifferent, or cynical, to imagine that anything that we say or do matters.

This book's first two sections delineated the words with which people hurt each other, the common words with which we express anger, criticism, and mockery. Words that heal are also "common"; they are words we already know, but don't use enough.

My friend editor Elisa Petrini once made this point via a telling question: "Who wouldn't recite a magical incantation if it would heal a loved one of a terrible illness? And yet ordinary nonmagical words just as certainly have the capacity to ease others' psychic ills." It's unfortunate that healing words often don't work their magic with the same speed as hurtful ones. One of life's unfair aspects is that hurtful words are usually far more potent than healing ones. Telling a child a hundred times, "I love you," or "You are the joy of my life" might not be powerful enough to overcome the long-term effects of a few outbursts like "What a fool (or idiot or dope) you are!" or "You're a selfish person who's never cared about anyone else!" or "What did I do that God punished me with you?" Often, to heal others, we need to reinforce again and again the positive message we give them. It's worth it.

Although most of us recognize the healing potential of words, we are often stingy about offering them. Consider the following exchange, which occurred at a Jewish funeral. After the service, everyone left the cemetery except for the mourning husband and the rabbi. The husband remained at the grave for a long while; finally, the rabbi approached him. "The service is long over, it is time for you to leave," he said.

The man waved him away. "You don't understand. I loved my wife."

"I am sure you did," the rabbi answered, "but you have been here a very long time. You should go now."

Again the husband said, "You don't understand. I loved my wife."

Once more the rabbi urged him to leave.

"But you don't understand," the man told him. "I loved my wife—and once, I almost told her."

When Jack Riemer, the rabbi from whom I heard this

story, finished, he added, "Can you imagine the sense of shame if you have to stand at a grave and bid farewell, and realize *then* what you didn't say when you *could* have, when you *should* have, when there was still time? Can you imagine having to live the rest of your life with the knowledge that you loved someone, and that 'once you almost told her'?"

Riemer's haunting story describes one of the commonest, and saddest, human traits. I term it "emotional constipation," an inability to express love, gratitude, and caring, even when these emotions are felt. The people who suffer from this malady are not necessarily incapable of expressing all emotions; many are quite adept at sharing anger and annoyance. Only when gentler emotions are called for do they become strangely reticent.

Why? For some, the reason why is often unresolved anger, or paralysis in the face of other people's needs. For others, it may be a lack of imagination, simply not knowing what to say. Now consider the case of Ian O'Gorman, a ten-year-old boy in Oceanside, California, who was diagnosed with cancer. The doctors prescribed ten weeks of chemotherapy, during which, they warned him, all his hair would fall out. To avoid the anxiety and pain of watching his hair gradually disappear, the youngster had his entire head shaved.

One can only imagine Ian's feelings a few days later when he returned to school, prematurely bald, and found that the thirteen other boys in his fifth-grade class, and their teacher as well, greeted him with their heads completely shaved.

What an eloquent statement of empathy! When the desire to ease someone else's pain is sufficiently deep, one can almost always find words or deeds that will make a difference.

Daily life calls for few such dramatic gestures. What others need from us, on an ongoing basis, is to know that they are cared for, that their good deeds inspire gratitude, and that others love them. It's that simple. And just because they hear such sentiments on Monday doesn't mean that they won't need to hear them again on Tuesday. This is the primary reason why words that heal and inspire must be repeated again and again.*

Rabbi Riemer once devoted his Yom Kippur sermon, the most important talk a rabbi gives during the year, to what he labeled "Four Phrases to Live By." He urged the synagogue's overflow crowd to "resolve that in this coming year you will learn to say four phrases more often than you have in the past:

"Thank you."

"I love you."

"How are you?"

"What do you need?"[2]

These four short statements and questions express gratitude, love, and caring, the three most important concerns that healing words can convey.

---

*Feeling responsible to speak healing words will seem difficult if you have to constantly remind yourself to invent kind things to say. Communicating such emotions then becomes an additional obligation in an already crowded life.

But if you understand that the words that heal people's pain, and that inspire and invigorate others, are only expressions of gratitude and love for what others have done for you, then healing words become much easier to express.

GRATITUDE

To become adept at saying "thank you," one must first cultivate gratitude; the Hebrew phrase for this, *ha-karat ha-tov,* literally means recognition of the good another has done you.

Such gratitude sometimes can be expressed by a simple "thank you," at other times by a lifetime of devotion.

Leopold Pfefferberg was one of the 1,100 Jews whom Oskar Schindler saved during the Holocaust. In 1947, just before Pfefferberg and his wife emigrated from Germany, he promised Schindler that he "would make his name known to the world." A short time later, when he learned that Schindler was impoverished, he helped raise $15,000 for him, a substantial amount of money in the late 1940s.

In 1950, Pfefferberg (who subsequently changed his name to Page) moved to Los Angeles and opened a leather-goods store in Beverly Hills, which many prominent Hollywood actors, writers, and producers patronized. He tried to interest them all in Schindler's story. On one occasion, when the wife of a prominent movie producer brought in two expensive handbags for repair, he told her, "If you let me talk to your husband about this story, you won't have to pay a penny for repairing the bags." The husband came in, and Pfefferberg told him about Schindler. Intrigued, the man wrote a treatment for a film, but unfortunately no studio was interested in producing it.

Pfefferberg was undaunted; throughout the 1960s and 1970s, he continued to tell everyone he could about Oskar Schindler. One day in October 1980, Australian novelist Thomas Keneally came into his store to buy a briefcase. When Pfefferberg learned that Keneally was a writer, he immediately started telling him Schindler's story and urged him to write a book about it.

Keneally listened attentively to Pfefferberg's recitation. He agreed that the story deserved to be told but added, "I am not the man who can write this book for you. . . . I was only three years old when the war started, so I don't know too much about it. Second, I am Catholic and don't know much about what happened to the Jews during the Holocaust. Third, I am not knowledgeable about Jewish suffering."

Fearful that yet another opportunity to fulfill his thirty-three-year-old vow to the now deceased Schindler would be lost, Pfefferberg was not dissuaded. "I was a teacher," he told Keneally, "and I lived through it. I will tell you everything I know. With a little research you will be as educated as anybody about this period of history. As an Irish Catholic and notable author you will have more credibility, not less, in writing about the Holocaust. You say you know nothing about Jewish suffering. . . . Irish people have suffered for four hundred years . . . [and] human suffering is the same, whether Jewish or Irish."

On the spot Keneally committed himself to writing the book. In 1982 *Schindler's List* was published to international acclaim. Pfefferberg subsequently served as a technical consultant to Steven Spielberg's 1994 Academy Award–winning film of the same title.

The promise a grateful Leopold Pfefferberg had made to Oskar Schindler in 1947 at last had been fulfilled. A man who also understood the meaning of gratitude, Keneally dedicated *Schindler's List* to Leopold Pfefferberg. And Steven Spielberg, also intent on expressing gratitude, concluded his film at the Catholic cemetery in Jerusalem, where he showed the surviving remnant of "Schindler's Jews" gathered around the righteous man's grave to honor his memory.

Of course, expressions of gratitude are usually carried out on a less grand scale. The Talmud teaches that "one who learns from his companion a single chapter, a single law, a single verse, a single expression, or even a single letter, should accord him respect."[3] In fulfillment of this teaching, when the third-century rabbinic sage Rav heard that his earliest childhood teacher had died, he tore his garment as a sign of mourning.[4] This act may seem exaggerated but, to one who appreciates the meaning of gratitude, it makes considerable sense. If you enjoy reading and appreciate that much of what you have been able to achieve in life derives from your literacy, then don't you owe a lifelong debt of gratitude to the person who taught you how to read?

In another teaching on gratitude, the Talmud speaks of the second-century rabbi Ben Zoma, who was grateful even to people he had never met but who had enriched his life. As Ben Zoma put it: "What labors did Adam [the first man on earth] have to carry out before he obtained bread to eat? He plowed, he sowed, he reaped, he bound the sheaves, threshed the grain, winnowed the chaff, selected the ears, ground them, sifted the flour, kneaded the dough, and baked. And only then did he eat. Whereas I get up and find all these things done for me."[5]

Jewish tradition ordains that a Jew should thank God with a hundred blessings every day. Although such a large number of blessings might strike some as "too much," a person who habituates him- or herself to recite blessings learns not to take life's pleasures for granted. Likewise, we should not take for granted the pleasures that others have provided for us.*

If *ha-karat ha-tov* means thanking the taxi driver who has driven well, acknowledging the waitress who has served you efficiently and pleasantly, and expressing gratitude to the bank official who has fulfilled a complex transaction graciously, then how much more gratitude do we owe our spouses, our children, and our parents—those who give meaning to our lives.

Rabbi Riemer's own years of clerical counseling inspired him to write "Things You Didn't Do," a poem describing the regrets of a woman who realized too late how stingy she had been in sharing her gratitude:

Remember the day I borrowed your brand new car and dented it?
I thought you'd kill me—but you didn't.

And remember the time I dragged you to the beach,
and you said it would rain, and it did?
I thought you would say, "I told you so,"—but you didn't.

*Contrast these descriptions of gratitude with Vice-President Alben Barkley's humorous, if admittedly hyperbolic, description of a disheartening conversation he had during his 1938 senatorial campaign in Kentucky: "I called on a certain rural constituent and was shocked to hear him say he was thinking of voting for my opponent. I reminded him of how many things I had done for him as a prosecuting attorney, as county judge, as congressman, and senator. I recalled how I had helped get an access road built to his farm, how I had visited him in a military hospital in France when he was wounded in the World War, how I had assisted him in securing his veteran's benefits, how I had arranged his loan from the Farm Credit Administration, how I had got him a disaster loan when the flood destroyed his home."

At the end of this lengthy recital, Barkley exhorted the constituent: "How can you think of voting for my opponent? Surely you remember all these things I have done for you?"

"Yeah," he said, "I remember. But what in hell have you done for me lately?"

And remember the time I flirted with all the guys
to make you jealous—and you were?
I thought you'd leave me—but you didn't.

And remember the time I spilled blueberry pie all
over your brand new rug?
I thought you'd drop me for sure—but you didn't. . . .

Yes, there are lots of things you didn't do,
But you put up with me, and you loved me, and you
protected me;

And there were so many things I wanted to make up
to you when you returned from the war—
but you didn't.[6]

In short, the people nearest to us should not be taken for granted, or made to wait for special occasions to hear our gratitude. Conveying appreciation is something we must do repeatedly. If we don't, we are, quite simply, ingrates.

WORDS OF LOVE

The second set of words that Riemer suggests we use more often is "I love you." Devoted parents of young children, and those involved in successful romantic relationships, know the importance of expressing these words, *often*. Unfortunately, many others either forget or neglect to say them, perhaps because they feel uncomfortable expressing tender emotions. There are so many ways to show our loving feelings. In her influential best-seller, *You Just Don't Understand: Women and Men in Conversation,* Deborah Tannen tells of her widowed great-aunt, who had a love affair while already in her seventies. Although the woman was overweight, balding, with hands and legs misshapen by arthritis, she had fallen in love with a man, also in his seventies, who would spend weekends in her apartment.

In describing to her great-niece what the relationship meant to her, the elderly woman recounted that she had gone out with friends for dinner and, when she returned home, her male companion telephoned. When she described the dinner to him, he listened with interest, then asked, "What did you wear?"

Recalling this question, Tannen's great-aunt started to cry. "Do you know how many years it's been since anyone asked me what I wore?"

"When my great-aunt said this," Tannen concluded, "she was saying that it had been years since anyone had cared deeply—intimately—about her." Because her great-aunt's companion cared deeply, he could find and express the words that made her feel loved.[7]

People who care about us have a right to know that they are loved. A woman once told me that she knew without a doubt that her mother-in-law loved her. But for some unexplainable reason the older woman never initiated a hug or kiss. In addition, her mother-in-law never complimented her, or noted her virtues. Instead, she showered the woman and her family with money and gifts. The middle-aged woman had a hurt and frightened look on her face as she told me her story. "All I would need is to hear her tell me once that she loved me. To know that all those years of distance were not personal. If she could just once tell me what it is she loves in me. Just once."

Love can be expressed in many ways, and a considerate person will strive to show it in the way the recipient needs. Professor Reuven Kimelman once told me: "Whether or not you have properly fulfilled the commandment of 'Love your neighbor as yourself' is proven not by your feeling that you have done so, but by your neighbor's feeling that you love him or her." For some people, love is primarily expressed through deeds. For others, loving words are what is most necessary. Those who act lovingly and speak lovingly bring joy to those around them and to themselves.

EXPRESSING CONCERN

The third and fourth phrases, "How are you?" and "What do you need?," put the emphasis on "you," on the needs and concerns of the person to whom we are speaking.

Joe Lapchick was one of the great basketball players in the pre–World War II era, and played center for the legendary original Celtics. When his young son was stricken with polio, Lapchick's neighbors expressed concern for the seven-year-old boy's health. The basketball star was shocked, however, when one of them, in the presence of the sick child, asked "if the boy would ever be able to play basketball again."

The next day, when he visited the hospital, he asked his son if he wanted to be a basketball player. The boy said yes, and his father told him that all he wanted was for him to have a happy and normal life, and to give something back to society.

The son eventually recovered and fortunately suffered no long-term effects from his illness. Years later, however, he still recalled the words his father had spoken to him that day in the hospital. As the son of a great athlete, he had always imagined that he had to follow in his father's footsteps. His father's words, which conveyed a love not conditioned on his son replicating his feats, freed the young boy from the complex that he too had to be a sports star: "I recognized . . . that my father had given me perhaps his greatest gift on that morning in Grasslands Hospital. He freed me of the need to please him and gave me the opportunity to fulfill myself."[8]

The Jewish tradition has constructed a myriad of ways to express concern to those most in need of it—people who've suffered the death of an immediate family member. The tradition instructs neighbors to have food prepared for the mourners when they return from the cemetery; in the absence of prepared foods, the Rabbis feared that depressed mourners would eat nothing at all. Those who visit mourners during the week following a death are instructed to remain silent until the mourner speaks. The visitor has no way of knowing what the mourner most needs at that moment. Thus, the visitor might feel that he must speak about the deceased, but the mourner might feel too emotionally overwrought to do so. Alternatively, the visitor might try to lighten the atmosphere by speaking of a movie or some other irrelevancy just when the mourner's most pressing need is to speak of the dead. And, of course, the mourner might just wish to sit quietly and say nothing. What matters is the mourner's needs.

Ascertaining what someone needs allows us to give him or her what is most meaningful and is thus, perhaps, the highest expression of love.

"I'M SORRY"

One additional phrase not on Rabbi Riemer's list is indispensable to any person who wishes to heal the hurt that she might have caused someone. Yet, for many people, "I'm sorry" are the hardest words to say. Apologizing means acknowledging that one has been wrong, perhaps even cruel.

We have all heard of feuds between siblings or close friends, quarrels that have lasted for years and which could have been brought to an immediate end if only one side had said, "I'm sorry."

If I seem to be exaggerating, then think of someone who has made you angry. In most cases, if that person suddenly came to your house, and sincerely expressed his remorse and sorrow at the hurt he had caused you, could you really remain unmoved?

According to an ancient Jewish teaching, a person who sincerely repents on Yom Kippur (the Day of Atonement) will be forgiven for any sins he or she has committed against God. But the Day of Atonement cannot bring about forgiveness for sins committed against another person until one goes to the person one has hurt and speaks healing words.

Put down this book for a moment now and think of someone you might have hurt, intentionally or unintentionally. If you are ready to do so, give the person a call and say, "I'm sorry."

If you are unwilling to do this, ask yourself why. Does it make sense to go on with the quarrel? Does the reason for the fight still seem as monumental as when it first occurred? If it doesn't, perhaps the time has come to write a letter of apology, or to call that person up and tell him, "I'm sorry for what I did. I'm sorry for our fight, sorry for our lost years of friendship."

According to the Talmud, one of the first questions the heavenly court addresses to those who have died is, "Did you hope for the world's redemption?" In other words, did you work toward leaving the world a better place than you found it? If you become the sort of person who learns to avoid speaking hurtful things about and to others, and accustom yourself to saying the words that buoy the spirits of those around you, you will have gone a long way toward fulfilling the age-old mission God addressed to humankind: "To perfect the world under the rule of God."

PART
FIVE

What Do We Do Now?

13

Incorporating the Principles of Ethical Speech into Daily Life

Recovering alcoholics know that, to succeed, they can never treat liquor casually. If they attend a party where liquor is served, they avoid it, realizing that just one sip can bring about catastrophic results. If they have joined AA, they gather with others to discuss common problems of remaining sober and to give each other reinforcement. They know that just making a mental or verbal commitment to stay sober won't work; what is required is unending vigilance.

Those who would speak ethically need to be equally determined to avoid hurting others with words. They must try to refrain from becoming involved in malicious gossip for even a minute or two, just as recovering alcoholics avoid taking even "one little sip." In some Orthodox Jewish communities, there are even support groups whose members encourage one another to refrain from speaking negatively of others.

For most of us, the best approach to ethical speech would be—to borrow from AA again—"one step at a time." What if, every day, for a two-hour period, we were particularly careful to say nothing bad about anyone. Perhaps lunch or dinner would be an ideal time, since often it is at mealtimes when much nasty gossip is spread and analyzed.

Another way to begin making ethical speech a part of your life is to review periodically the principles discussed in this book. I suspect that many of you have nodded in agreement at many of the observations and anecdotes. Perhaps you've concluded that it's wrong to disseminate negative and/or ugly truths about others, to spread cruel and reputation-destroying rumors, and to introduce irrelevant, embarrassing information into a quarrel. You may be determined to refrain from ranting and raving in response to minor provocations, and to desist from humiliating others.

Yet, if you're like me, it's unlikely that reading this book once will "cure" you of the tendency to use words unkindly, any more than one reading of a powerful book on the horrors of drunkenness will induce an alcoholic to become permanently sober.

For most of us, gossiping and talking to others unfairly are about as addictive as liquor is for alcoholics. Thus, if you wish to change the way you speak *about* and *to* people, you need to practice consistently the principles outlined on the following pages.

ON GOSSIP THAT IS TRIVIAL AND TRUE

When you make comments, even positive ones, about someone, remember how easily the conversation can drift in negative directions. A remark such as "I think Chuck is great, but there's one thing I can't stand about him" is unlikely to trigger an extended discussion of Chuck's good attributes; rather, the conversation probably will focus on that "one thing."

Whenever you find yourself involved in an innocuous conversation about someone but negative comments begin to be made, remember Oliver Sipple's fate. He saved the president's life, became an overnight hero, and was the subject of many positive news stories. Yet Sipple's new status subjected him to such devastating personal scrutiny that by the time it ended, his life had been ruined, permanently.

NEGATIVE TRUTHS (*LASHON HA-RA*)

In probably no other area of life do so many of us regularly violate the Golden Rule, as in speaking negative truths. If you were about to enter a room and heard the people inside talking about you, what would you least like to hear? Wouldn't it be a description of your character flaws and/ or the intimate details of your personal life? Yet when we gossip about others, those are the very things that are most likely to come up.

Is it difficult to avoid gossiping about the ugly parts of other people's lives? Definitely. It has always been, and always will be, because few things are more interesting to talk about than other people's flaws, private hurts, and scandals.

If you wish to treat others with the kindness you would have them extend to you, recall *before* you speak the advice of Jonathan K. Lavater, the eighteenth-century Swiss theologian and poet: "Never tell evil of a man if you do not know it for a certainty, and if you know it for a certainty, then ask yourself, 'Why should I tell it?' "

Occasionally, you may have a valid reason to say something negative about another person. For example, if somebody wants to go into business with, or hire, or is dating someone you know to be inappropriate for him or her, you should tell that person—*but no one else*—what you know. When doing so, *don't* exaggerate. And if you're not certain that the information is true, say so: "I've heard it said that . . . but I'm not sure it's true; I just think you should look into it."

Be specific about why you think the person is inappropriate for the individual to whom you're speaking. Avoid statements like "There is a very good reason you shouldn't hire him. I can't tell you why but, believe me, don't hire him."

This type of declaration almost always is unfair to the person about whom you're speaking: Similarly, it would be wrong to say to someone, "I don't want to have anything to do with you anymore, but I can't tell you why."

When I was a child, my father once overheard my mother reading to me the children's rhyme:

> I do not love you, Dr. Fell
> But why I cannot tell,
> But this I know full well
> I do not love you, Dr. Fell.

My father interrupted my mother to point out: "That's a terribly cruel poem. The person who is speaking is being very unfair to Dr. Fell."

Remember: Even in those instances when it's permissible to spread a negative truth, be specific, be precise, and be fair.

In other cases, when the negative information is no one else's business, let the words of Ben Sira, a wise citizen of ancient Israel, guide you: "Have you heard something? Let it die with you. Be strong; it will not burst you" (Apocrypha, *Ecclesiasticus* 19:10).

RUMORS AND LIES (*MOTZI SHEM RA*)

Throughout history, rumors and lies probably have caused as much misery as war. Over the millennia, lies about the Jews—that they caused the Black Plague by poisoning Europe's wells, drank the blood of non-Jews at their religious rituals, or were involved in an international conspiracy to take over the world and enslave gentiles—have led to the murder of millions of innocent people.

Similarly, lies and rumors destroy the lives of individuals. Iago's fabrications caused Othello to murder Desdemona, and a twelve-year-old girl's lie, conveyed by rumormongers, prompted a woman to commit suicide in *The Children's Hour.*

Before spreading a negative report, remember the Talmud's words: "If something is as clear to you as the fact that your sister is sexually forbidden to you, [only] then say it."

And even in such a case, speak only to those who need the information. In those instances when you feel it important to pass on a rumor (for example, someone is contemplating investing funds with a person you have heard is dishonest), emphasize that your information is unconfirmed and requires further investigation.

ANGER

Dr. Solomon Schimmel, a Boston psychologist and psychotherapist, reports that "I spend more time helping clients deal with their anger than with any other emotion."[1]

Anger is a very common, powerful emotion. Yet as difficult as it is to control *what* makes us angry, we can generally control *how* we express our feelings. If you have made comments while angry that you subsequently regretted, or that might have ended a relationship, observing a simple rule may well guarantee that you never do so again: *Limit the expression of your anger to the incident that provoked it.*

If you do choose to share your anger with others, avoid doing so with individuals who will inflame your feelings ("He said *that* to you? That's disgusting. What are you going to do about it?") Rather, choose people who are apt to calm you and help you put things in a broader perspective.

Above all, remember that the most important person with whom you should speak is the one with whom you're angry. As psychologist Carol Tavris has written: "If you are angry at Ludwig, all the discussions in the world with your best friend will not solve the problem." Indeed, if your antagonist hears that you've been speaking ill of him or her to others, that individual's anger probably will grow, and make reconciliation between the two of you much more difficult.

FIGHTING FAIR

When it comes to football, Vince Lombardi may have been right (although I think not) in the statement attributed to him: "Winning is the only thing."

But when it comes to conflicts between people, no advice could be more harmful. People who believe that winning an argument, particularly a personal one, is "the only thing" are likely to introduce unfair points into disputes, and to end relationships. Remember: *Never bring in information about the person with whom you are arguing to discredit or embarrass him or her.* That's what Rabbi Yochanan did to Resh Lakish when he publicly reminded everyone witnessing their dispute that Resh Lakish once had been a thief. This nongermane and unfair information led to a permanent, tragic rupture in the two men's friendship.

Through repeated questioning of audiences over the years, I have learned that perhaps half or more of all families have close relatives who no longer are on speaking terms. Almost invariably, the rift started with an argument that escalated, with one or both parties saying increasingly harsh things. The time to avoid making ugly comments is *before* they leave your mouth. Once they do, the other party might forgive; it is unlikely that he or she will forget. Would you?

HOW TO CRITICIZE

Before you criticize somebody, ask yourself three questions:

1. *How do I feel about offering this criticism? Does it give me pleasure or pain?*

If part of you is looking forward to it, hold back. Your motives are probably at least partly insincere (you don't so much wish to help the person as relish cutting him down to size) and your listener will probably respond defensively and reject your critique.

If the thought of criticizing another pains you, yet you feel impelled to speak up, do so. Your motives probably are sincere; your concern for the other person will shine through, making it likely that he or she will be able to accept, or at least hear, your criticism.

2. *Does my criticism offer specific ways to change?*

3. *Are my words nonthreatening and reassuring?*

When criticizing, avoid the words "always" ("You're always irresponsible") and "never" ("You've never thought about anyone else's needs"). Such words one-dimensionalize and demoralize the person being criticized and will probably impel her to deny *everything* you're saying. Who would admit, "Yes, it's true. I've *never* thought about anyone else's needs"? Be particularly careful to avoid speaking such words to children. Their egos tend to be especially vulnerable, and such rebukes could result in their feeling worthless. Keep in mind the words of Johann Paul Friedrich: "If a child tells a lie, tell him that he has told a lie, but don't call him a liar. If you define him as a liar, you break down his confidence in his own character."

When offering criticism, think strategically: Remember

the three suggestions of Moses Maimonides, the medieval Jewish philosopher and rabbi:

"He who rebukes another . . . should

1. administer the rebuke in private,

2. speak to the offender gently and tenderly, and

3. point out that he is only speaking for the wrong-doer's own good."

LEARNING HOW TO ACCEPT CRITICISM

Because we are capable of improving, and otherwise growing, we should regard those who criticize us *fairly* and *constructively* with the same gratitude we feel toward a physician who accurately diagnoses an ailment. Without the diagnosis, we would remain sick and likely grow sicker; without the critic's words, we might deteriorate ethically.

So when someone criticizes you, resist the temptation to point out similar or other flaws in her, whether they exist or not. Instead, ask yourself: *"Is what she is saying true?"* If her criticism seems overstated, then ask yourself another question: *"Is there any validity in the criticism? Can I take what she has said and use it to improve myself?"*

PUBLIC HUMILIATION

Jewish law regards humiliating another person, particularly in public, as one of the cruelest things one can do. Public humiliation is a trauma from which few people ever recover, as exemplified by the seven-year-old girl whose teacher publicly ridiculed her before the whole class, the overweight adolescent whose mother mocked her in front of visiting relatives and friends, and the rape victim confronted by a criminal defense lawyer who tried to convince the jury that she was a part-time prostitute.

Because public humiliation often inflicts irrevocable damage, it sometimes can be unforgivable. To avoid ever humiliating another person again, there are two things you must do:

Reflect again and again on the moral evil of shaming another person. This is particularly important for those people who possess both quick tempers and sharp wits. This combination sometimes tempts them to make clever, but very hurtful, wisecracks at other people's expense (unfortunately, it's much harder to be clever when praising someone). A Yiddish witticism teaches: "Who is a hero? One who suppresses a wisecrack."

When you're upset, think before you speak.

Once, an old rabbi witnessed a young man admonishing another. Because the rebuke was tactless and very sharp, the face of the man being criticized turned red.

The rabbi stopped the admonisher, took him aside, and informed him that he was committing a far more serious sin than had been committed by the other man.

The rebuker took offense at the rabbi's words. "What that man did was so wrong that he deserves to be humiliated, *even if it costs me my share in the World-to-Come.*"

The old rabbi later confided: "At that moment, I wondered if this young man even believed in the World-to-Come. When calm, I don't think he would have been willing to sacrifice his little finger, let alone all eternity, for the sake of delivering his rebuke. Yet, when angry, people are capable of making insane pronouncements."

Although angry people are the ones who are most likely to humiliate others, the Talmud warns us all to be careful not to do so: "If somebody was hanged in a person's family, don't say to him, 'Hang up this fish for me,' " lest the comment set off a painful memory or remind others present of the disgrace. If the Talmud is concerned about so improbable a case, how much more must we take care not to mock another's bad breath, acne, physical unattractiveness, lack of intelligence, or failure to achieve professional success.

IS LYING ALWAYS WRONG?

In interpersonal relations, truth is a very important, but not always the highest, value. Although Immanuel Kant thought it preferable to let a murderer kill someone rather than lie to him about the would-be victim's whereabouts, ethical common sense and love of humankind dictate that some lies are justified, not only when life is at stake, but also when telling the truth would inflict pain without gain. Thus, if somebody who is going to a social gathering and is dressed inappropriately asks you: "How do I look?," answer honestly. Advising him to change his clothes might be momentarily awkward, but will save him far greater embarrassment. But if you meet a person at a party who is inappropriately dressed, and she asks you: "How do I look?" it would be pointless and cruel to say "terrible," or "totally inappropriate."

However, it's wrong to tell a lie when your goal is not to avoid inflicting pain, but to secure personal advantage. For example, it is wrong to make a "big show" of inviting someone to be your guest when you know he or she will refuse, just so that the person will think of you as a devoted friend. Jewish thought regards this as a form of stealing (that is, you are "stealing" a good name under false pretenses).

Regarding "macro" issues, lying is virtually always wrong; even when told to promote a noble cause, untruths are apt to lead to unforeseen and immoral consequences. Remember, the Allied propagandists who spread lies about German atrocities during World War I may have succeeded in strengthening anti-German feelings throughout the West. But they inadvertently helped inspire Adolf Hitler to tell his big lies before and during World War II, while also leading others to believe that the reports of Nazi atrocities might also be mere propaganda.

Also immoral is the untruth spread by some zealous feminists that 150,000 American women die annually of anorexia nervosa, an eating disorder they blame on men and the misogynistic culture they have created (in actuality, about fifty to a hundred American women die annually of anorexia). This untruth has caused some women to become unfairly furious at men, many of whom deeply love female family members and friends who have anorexia, and are extremely pained by their suffering.

Such lies ultimately also are unfortunate for their promoters, for once people learn that someone has misled them, they are less likely to believe other, perhaps true, claims that person makes.

Remember the words of Friedrich Hebbel (a nineteenth-century German playwright): "One lie does not cost you one truth, but *the* truth."

IF YOU ARE GOING TO GOSSIP ANYWAY, IS IT STILL WORTH READING THIS BOOK?

Emphatically, yes. The Talmud, with its realistic assessment of human nature, suggests that almost everyone, even a person with the best intentions, utters a "negative truth" at least once daily.

Reviewing the principles of ethical speech regularly will achieve one important effect: Although you may still gossip, you will do less of it. And you will probably be less cruel in discussing others.

If you do gossip, severely limit the amount of time you spend doing so, and restrict your comments to a spouse (or a close boyfriend or girlfriend) and perhaps one or two close friends.

When I suggested this to an acquaintance, he responded: "But isn't it true that once you gossip at all, you're violating the principles of ethical speech, so what does it matter if you gossip a lot or a little?"

I answered: "If you tell me that you're driving tonight and you plan to speed, I'll urge you to drive at sixty miles per hour rather than one hundred. At one hundred miles per hour, your violation of the law is much greater, and much worse things are likely to happen."

In short, when it comes to ethical behavior, you should

make an effort to make yourself and other people better, even when you know that you and they aren't going to strive for perfection.

Finally, as you try to restrain yourself from spreading a juicy bit of gossip or directing a stinging remark, remember Rabbi Harold Kushner's words: "Only God can give us credit for the angry [or other cruel] words we did not speak."[2]

14

Where Heaven and Earth Touch:
A National "Speak No Evil Day"

What if we could share our consciousness of the power of words with many others—even the whole nation?

Tens of millions of Americans annually observe "The Great American Smokeout" and "Earth Day," one concerned with eliminating pollution of our bodies, the other the pollution of our planet. A national "Speak No Evil Day" could work to eliminate the pollution of our emotional atmosphere, the realm in which we interact with others.

I envision "Speak No Evil Day" as being observed on May 14, starting in 1996. Indeed, Senators Connie Mack of Florida and Joseph Lieberman of Connecticut have introduced a resolution in the U.S. Senate to establish such a day (see page 187 for the text of that resolution).

"Speak No Evil Day" would have both short- and

long-term goals: to eliminate all vicious and unfair talk for twenty-four hours, and thus plant the seed of a more permanent shift in our consciousness.

On this day people will attempt to refrain from saying a single nasty comment about others, even if true. Only in the very rare instances when it's absolutely necessary to transmit negative information will they do so. Otherwise, like those who engage in periodic cleansing fasts to purify their bodies, people will go for an entire day without uttering unfair and hurtful talk.

On this day people also will monitor and regulate how they speak to others. Everyone will strive to keep his or her anger under control. If a person does express anger, he will do so fairly, and limit his comments to the incident that provoked his ire. People likewise will argue fairly, and not allow their disputes to degenerate into name-calling or other forms of verbal abuse. No one, not even a person offering deserved criticism, will humiliate another.

In short, on "Speak No Evil Day," people will strive to fulfill the Golden Rule, and will speak about others with the same kindness and fairness that they wish others to exercise when speaking about them.

I hope that journalists and other media professionals will be touched by the spirit of the day. While retaining the right to report *relevant* negative items about public figures, they will omit innuendos, sarcastic asides, rumors, and the publicizing of private scandals.

On "Speak No Evil Day," all of us will refrain from disseminating rumors, particularly negative ones.

On this day too, people will strive to avoid hurting and defaming groups as well as individuals. By avoiding bigoted sweeping comments—even for one day—we may finally come to view others as individuals, and realize that negative stereotypes of large ethnic, religious, racial and gender groups are unfair and untrue.

A rabbi once told me that his grandmother used to say, "It is not within everyone's power to be beautiful, but all of us can make sure that the words that come out of our mouths are."

"Speak No Evil Day" will be a twenty-four-hour period of verbal beauty:

—It will be a day when a young child frequently teased by his classmates, and called by an ugly nickname, can go to school confident no one will say a cruel word to him.

—It will be a day on which an employee with a sharp-tongued boss can go to work without fearing that he or she will be verbally abused.

—It will be a day on which that sharp-tongued boss, the type who says, "I don't get ulcers, I give them," might come to understand how vicious such a statement is, and will say nothing that will cause pain.

—It will be a day when a fat adolescent will not have to fear a biting comment about his weight from parents or peers.

—It will be a day when a man who once served a prison sentence but who has led an exemplary life since being released will not have to fear that a journalist will publicize his earlier behavior.

—It will be a day when a congressional candidate who suffered a nervous breakdown will not have to worry that his opponent will use this painful episode to publicly humiliate him.

—It will be a day when an African American or Hispanic American can be among other Americans without fearing that she will hear prejudicial comments or ugly words about herself or her racial group.

—It will be a day when a husband who usually only tells his wife his complaints will tell her instead that he loves her and why.

—It will be a day when people will use the words that heal others' emotional wounds, not those that inflict them.

In short, "Speak No Evil Day" will be a day when, through humankind's collective efforts, we will experience a taste of heaven on earth.

A Jewish proverb teaches: "If you will it, it is no fantasy." If we only want it enough, "Speak No Evil Day" is possible. Let us try.

Appendix

TEXT OF SENATE RESOLUTION TO ESTABLISH A NATIONAL "SPEAK NO EVIL DAY"

On July 17, 1995, Senator Connie Mack of Florida submitted, on behalf of himself and Senator Joseph Lieberman of Connecticut, the following resolution to the first session of the 104th Congress:

RESOLUTION

To designate May 16, 1996, and May 14, 1997, as "National Speak No Evil Day," and for other purposes.

Whereas words used unfairly, whether expressed through excessive anger, unfair criticism, public and private humiliation, bigoted comments, cruel jokes, or rumors and malicious gossip, traumatize and destroy many lives;

Whereas an unwillingness or inability of many parents to control what they say when angry causes the infliction of often irrevocably damaging verbal abuse on the children;

Whereas bigoted words are often used to dehumanize entire religious, racial, and ethnic groups, and inflame hostility in a manner that may lead to physical attacks;

Whereas the spreading of negative, often unfair, untrue or exaggerated, comments or rumors about others often inflicts irrevocable damage on the victim of the gossip, the damage epitomized in the expression "character assassination";

Whereas the inability of a person to refrain for 24 hours from speaking unkind and cruel words demonstrates a lack of control as striking as the inability of an alcoholic to refrain for 24 hours from drinking liquor; Now therefore, be it

Resolved, That the Senate designates May 14, 1996, and May 14, 1997, as "National Speak No Evil Day." The Senate requests that the President issue a proclamation calling on the people of the United States to observe the days with appropriate ceremonies and activities, including educational endeavors.

Notes

INTRODUCTION

1. Jewish law labels such speech *ona'at devarim*, "wronging with words," and regards it as a serious offense.

2. Even the child who chants "Sticks and stones" knows that words and names *can* hurt him or her: The statement usually is an attempt at bravado by a child who more likely feels like crying. The early twentieth-century poem "Incident," by the African-American poet Countee Cullen, provides a powerful poetic depiction of the power of words to hurt:

> *Once riding in old Baltimore,*
> *Heart-filled, head-filled with glee*
> *I saw a Baltimorean*
> *Keep looking straight at me.*
>
> *Now I was eight and very small*
> *And he was no whit bigger,*
> *And so I smiled, but he poked out*
> *His tongue, and called me, "Nigger."*
>
> *I saw the whole of Baltimore*
> *From May until December;*
> *Of all the things that happened there*
> *That's all that I remember.*

3. *Sachar Tov*, #120; I am following the translation cited in Earl Schwartz, *Moral Development: A Practical Guide for Jewish Teachers* (Denver: Alternatives in Religious Education Publications, 1983), p. 78. This book contains a particularly valuable chapter (pp. 71–82) on how to teach children to refrain from gossiping, slandering, and shaming others.

Part One: *The Unrecognized Power of Words*

CHAPTER 1: THE UNRECOGNIZED POWER OF WORDS

1. Throughout history, words have proven father to the deed. The Nazis and their collaborators would have been unlikely to succeed in carrying out the Holocaust were it not for the centuries-long legacy of anti-Jewish words, expressions, and writings that they inherited. Among those were *The Protocols of the Elders of Zion*; the expression popularized in 1879 by the German historian Heinrich von Treitschke, "The Jews are our misfortune," which became the Nazis' slogan; and, of course, the infamous term "Christ-killer," a legacy of Christian antisemitism.

2. Rush Limbaugh, *The Ways Things Ought to Be* (New York: Pocket Books, paperback, 1992), pp. 194, 204.

3. Cited in Dennis Prager, "Liberals and the Decline of Dialogue," *Ultimate Issues* (January–March 1990), p. 11.

4. Cited in Ethan Bronner, *Battle for Justice: How the Bork Nomination Shook America* (New York: W. W. Norton, 1982), p. 98. See the discussion of the attacks on Bork in Stephen Carter, *The Confirmation Mess* (New York: Basic Books, 1994), pp. 45–50. Carter, a law professor at Yale, and himself a liberal, writes: "It is plain that the campaign to defeat [Bork] lifted snippets of his scholarship and his judicial decisions very far out of their contexts, distorting or misleading to raise popular ire" (p. 45). As regards Senator Kennedy's attack, Carter writes that it "was surely beyond the pale" (p. 50).

5. Cited in Michael Medved, *Hollywood vs. America* (New York: Harper-Collins; Zondervan, 1992), p. 194.

6. Ibid., pp. 150, 193.

7. Ibid., p. 150.

8. *Washington Post*, May 13, 1992.

Part Two: How We Speak About Others

CHAPTER 2: THE IRREVOCABLE DAMAGE INFLICTED BY
GOSSIP

1. Babylonian Talmud, *Berakhot* 58a.

2. Stephen Bates, *If No News, Send Rumors: Anecdotes of American Journalism*
(New York: Henry Holt, 1989), pp. 142–143. I am omitting the name of
the reporter who originally publicized the information in the *Los Angeles
Times.*

. 3. American law, it should be noted, does protect citizens from "invasion
of privacy." Thus, a newspaper is forbidden to pick out a name at random
from a telephone book and assign reporters to write an "exposé" about the
person. Arguing that the reporters had invaded his privacy, Sipple sued the
newspapers. The suit was eventually dismissed on the grounds that by intervening to save the president's life, Sipple had in essence become a "public
figure"; hence, he no longer was exempt from having his privacy invaded.
How apt seems the cynical proverb "No good deed goes unpunished."

4. Despite Churchill's vigorous denial, one still finds this nasty quip commonly attributed to him in anthologies, providing yet another example of
how impossible it is to recover all the feathers once they've been scattered
to the wind.

5. Ed Koch, *Citizen Koch: An Autobiography* (New York: St. Martin's Press,
1992), pp. 248–249.

6. *Washington Post,* March 2, 1989.

7. Cited in Larry Sabato, *Feeding Frenzy: How Attack Journalism Has Transformed American Politics* (New York: Free Press, 1991), p. 181. During the
same period that Woodward's article appeared, Sabato notes that CBS-TV
correspondent Lesley Stahl reported on ."a drunken encounter between
Tower and a Russian-born dancing school owner." She acknowledged that
the FBI was "unable to corroborate any of the story, and we were unable
to corroborate it as well." But the item, so damning to Tower, and apparently also untrue, was relayed to millions of viewers. Many undoubtedly
assumed that the story was true, for why else would Stahl report it on the
CBS Evening News?

8. A short, insightful overview and discussion of the Tower episode is found in Adrian Havill, *Deep Truth: The Lives of Bob Woodward and Carl Bernstein* (New York: Carol Publishing, 1993), p. 209.

9. Babylonian Talmud, *Shabbat* 145b.

10. *USA Today,* May 18, 1994, p. 1.

11. Indeed, the victim often wishes that he or she were dead. New York's former mayor Ed Koch devoted a lifetime to creating an image of himself as an idealistic and honest, if somewhat ornery, civil servant. Yet during his third term, a number of reporters exposed several instances of Koch appointees' acting dishonestly. When some suggested that the illegalities reached into the mayor's office as well, Koch was thrown into a profound depression. In his memoirs, *Citizen Koch,* he reports that although he knew he wasn't a thief, he realized that many people who read the articles would conclude otherwise: "My integrity was the most important thing to me; *my good name meant more to me than anything else I had.* . . . I never minded if people disliked me for the positions I took, or for the things I said, but I simply could not accept that people might think I was dishonest" (emphasis mine).

He recalled: "It was a very painful time. There were even moments when I thought seriously of killing myself. I really did. I thought about it in tactical terms, and I thought about it in spiritual terms. . . . If only I had a gun. Thank God I had convinced Bob McGuire [the police commissioner] to remove the gun from my bathroom safe all those years ago. If I had had it, at that vulnerable point, I really think I might have used it. A gun would have done the job nicely, cleanly, quickly. I think it's entirely possible that if I had a gun nearby, in the spring and summer of 1986, I would not be here today . . . in my weakest moment, I might have just determined to get the whole ordeal over with" (*Citizen Koch,* pp. 212–214).

Although he overcame the impulse to kill himself, Koch is convinced that the anxiety generated by the malicious attacks on his character contributed significantly to his 1987 stroke. Fortunately, it eventually became clear that the mayor had engaged in no dishonest activities, and his good name was restored. But at what a cost!

12. Hellman did not use fiction to create a wildly exaggerated morality tale on the perils of a vicious tongue. Rather, she based her story on an event

that had occurred in Edinburgh in 1809, and which British writer William Roughead chronicled in a 1930 book, *Bad Companions*.

13. I read this somewhere, but unfortunately don't remember who said it. I would appreciate a reader sending me information as to the author of this statement.

CHAPTER 3: THE LURE OF GOSSIP

1. Babylonian Talmud, *Ta'anit* 8a.

2. Shakespeare likewise put the statement in the mouth of a "snake" (albeit one in human form), Iago, the villain of *Othello*.

3. Occasionally, there could be a financial motive for spreading gossip, as in the case of a business owner who disseminates stories about a competitor with the hope of driving him or her out of business.

4. At one point during 1992, three of the fifteen books on the *New York Times*'s nonfiction best-seller list were detailed accounts of Charles and Diana's miserably unhappy marriage. Another possible reason for the intense curiosity about the royal couple: Diana's predicament reminded both adults and children of childhood fairy tales about unhappy princesses; millions of men undoubtedly fantasized that they could inspire in Diana the love her royal husband could not.

5. Samuel Warren and Louis Brandeis, "The Right to Privacy," *Harvard Law Review*, December 15, 1890; reprinted in Tom Goldstein, ed., *Killing the Messenger: 100 Years of Media Criticism* (New York: Columbia University Press, 1989), p. 9.

6. Deborah Tannen, *You Just Don't Understand: Women and Men in Conversation* (New York: William Morrow, 1990; Ballantine Books, paperback 1991), p. 107.

7. Alan Dershowitz, *Chutzpah* (Boston: Little, Brown, 1991), p. 15. The only note that strikes a somewhat false chord in this story is Dershowitz's assumption that the gossipmonger was relieved to learn that so prominent a Jew had not intermarried; if nothing else, such knowledge deprived her of a juicy bit of gossip. On the other hand, the fact that she could now tell an anecdote recounting her "friendship" and conversation with Mrs.

Dershowitz, mother of the well-known professor and attorney, might have been sufficient compensation for no longer being able to spread an untrue bit of gossip.

8. Jack Levin and Arnold Arluke, *Gossip: The Inside Scoop* (New York: Plenum Press, 1987). pp. 14–16. Levin and Arluke undertook no further study of the personalities or motives of the respondents who claimed to have attended the wedding that never occurred. But they cite another study of people who spread false gossip, albeit unknowingly. Social psychologists Ralph Rosnow and Gary Fine investigated the 1969 rumor, spread largely on college campuses, that Beatles star Paul McCartney had died and that the Beatles were keeping his death a secret. They discovered that the people who initially circulated this story generally were less popular, dated less often, and had fewer friends than those who rejected the rumor and/or didn't spread it. As Levin and Arluke summarize the study's conclusion: "Because gossip often places people at the center of attention, it also, at least temporarily, enhances their status with others. This may explain why gossipmongers come from the most isolated, least popular members of a group. After all, they are the ones who most need something to make them socially acceptable" (p. 16; the Rosnow and Fine study is published in "Inside Rumors," *Human Behavior* [1974], pp. 64–68).

9. Babylonian Talmud, *Bava Bathra* 164b. The first view expressed in the Talmud is that every person speaks negative truths (*lashon ha-ra*) every day. This view is challenged, and the Rabbis then say that, at the very least, every person speaks "the dust of *lashon ha-ra*" daily. For examples of what constitutes such "dust," see page 23.

CHAPTER 4: WHEN, IF EVER, IS IT APPROPRIATE TO REVEAL INFORMATION THAT WILL HUMILIATE OR HARM ANOTHER?

1. Haffetz Hayyim, *Shmirat ha-Lashon* (Guarding One's Tongue), 4:1; I have followed, with minor variations, Rabbi Alfred Cohen's translation in "Privacy: A Jewish Perspective," in Alfred S. Cohen, ed., *Halacha and Contemporary Society* (New York: Ktav, 1984), pp. 234–235.

2. Cohen, ibid., pp. 213–218.

3. Rabbi Cohen's ruling is based on the broad application Jewish law gives to the biblical verse "Do not stand by while your neighbor's blood is shed" (Leviticus 19:16); see page 54.

4. Rabbi Alfred S. Cohen, "On Maintaining a Professional Confidence," *The Journal of Halacha and Contemporary Society*, VII (Spring 1984), pp. 73–87.

5. Ibid., p. 78.

6. Although doctor-patient confidentiality almost always should be protected, a physician who learns that a patient is HIV-positive (or already has AIDS) must insist that the person inform his or her spouse and/or past and present sexual partners. If the patient doesn't do so, the doctor is *morally* obligated to inform those people who might be infected by the patient's potentially fatal virus. (Whether American medical ethics *legally* permits him to do so is the source of considerable controversy.) This is based once again on the principle of biblical ethics: "Do not stand by while your neighbor's blood is shed" (Leviticus 19:16; see page 54). Important as doctor-patient confidentiality is, it is a less compelling value than saving a person's life.

7. A broad outline of the Tarasoff case, and the various justices' opinions, is found in "Tarasoff *vs.* the Regents of the University of California et al.," in Richard A. Wasserstrom, ed., *Today's Moral Problems*, 3rd ed. (New York: Macmillan, 1985), pp. 243–262. The reasoning of Justice Matthew Tobriner, ruling for the majority, strikes me as morally just: "The risk that unnecessary warnings be given is a reasonable price to pay for the lives of possible victims that may be saved. We would hesitate to hold that the therapist who is aware that his patient expects to attempt to assassinate the president of the United States would not be obligated to warn the authorities because the therapist cannot predict with accuracy that his patient will commit the crime."

8. It seems to me that had Drs. Moore and Powelson followed my proposed guideline, there is a good chance Tatiana Tarasoff never would have been murdered. Undoubtedly, if Poddar had confided to Moore his intent to kill Moore's family members, the doctor would have warned them against Poddar. And had Moore, in such a case, solicited Dr. Powelson's advice, I doubt that Powelson would have instructed him not to reveal the threats to anyone, including his family members.

9. At the end of the film, a jury finds the priest not guilty, although the whole town assumes he is. The murderer's wife, shocked at the cruelty the townspeople are displaying to the priest, blurts out that she knows him to be innocent. At this point, her husband murders her, and the priest's reputation is saved. Unfortunately, by then the cost in both innocent life and ruined reputations has been very great.

10. In an indirect reference to the secrecy of the confession, the murderer says to the priest, Father Koesler, "I had to tell someone. Somebody who couldn't tell anybody else." See William X. Kienzle, *The Rosary Murders* (New York: Random House, paperback, 1985), p. 175. Father Hoesler feels compelled to solve the crime himself, but without utilizing any of the information he gained during confession. Unfortunately, more innocent people are murdered before he succeeds, deaths that likely would have been averted had the priest revealed what he had learned during confession.

11. Ibid., p. 176.

CHAPTER 5: PRIVACY AND PUBLIC FIGURES

1. Stephen Bates, *If No News, Send Rumors: Anecdotes of American Journalism* (New York: Henry Holt, 1989), p. 150. Bates's book is a fascinating collection of several hundred anecdotes, many of them detailing instances of irresponsible and immoral journalism.

2. David Nyberg, *The Varnished Truth: Truth Telling and Deceiving in Ordinary Life* (Chicago: University of Chicago Press, 1992), p. 129.

3. Charles Fried, "Privacy," *Yale Law Journal* 77 (1968), p. 477.

4. Larry Sabato's *Feeding Frenzy: How Attack Journalism Has Transformed American Politics* (New York: Free Press, 1991), a study of the impact of what the author calls "attack journalism" on American political life, cites thirty-six years of Gallup Poll samplings of Americans' opinions of the Democratic and Republican presidential candidates. One question measures the combined rate of "very favorable" impressions respondents gave the nominees:

1952—84%
1956—94%
1960—77%

1964—76%
1968—63%
1972—63%
1976—69%
1980—51%
1984—68%
1988—42%

The average "very favorable" rating between 1952–1964 was 83 percent; since 1968 it has declined to 59 percent. Sabato notes that while it is true that many of the unfortunate events that occurred during these years are precisely the sort that provoke cynicism (the Vietnam War, Watergate, the Iran hostage crisis), "This period of growing cynicism coincides almost precisely with the new era of freewheeling 'anything goes' journalism" (pp. 207–208).

As an example of journalistic excess, media analyst Stephen Bates reports that in 1987, "*The New York Times* asked each presidential candidate for copies of medical and psychiatric records, school records, (including high school grades), birth certificates, marriage and driver's licenses, employment records, financial statements, tax returns, and lists of closest friends . . . it [also] asked the candidates to waive their rights of privacy to any confidential files the FBI and CIA kept on them" (*If No News, Send Rumors,* p. 124). At the time, *Chicago Tribune* columnist Mike Royko called a *Times* spokesperson and asked her to supply similar information about the newspaper's editor. She hung up on him. The *Times* subsequently backed off from its demand for FBI and CIA files, and for medical records unrelated to "fitness for the presidency."

5. Larry Sabato, *Feeding Frenzy,* pp. 207–208. Many examples in this chapter are taken from this extraordinarily thorough, thoughtful study of the impact of intrusive journalism on American life.

6. In addition to circumstantial evidence that Judith Exner served as a courier between John Kennedy and Sam Giancana, there is also reason to believe that the mobster contributed substantial sums to Kennedy's election campaign. If these allegations are true, and there is compelling evidence they are (ibid., p. 34), this incident provides a rare instance of a sexual liaison that *was* the public's business.

7. William Safire, cited in Sabato, op. cit., p. 35.

8. In Anthony Summers, *The Secret Life of J. Edgar Hoover* (New York: Pocket Books, 1994), pp. 61ff, the author reports that as late as 1966 Hoover said scornfully of blacks, "Instead of saying, 'Boy, come here!' they want to be addressed as Mr."

9. Dennis Prager in *Ultimate Issues* (January–March 1992), p. 13.

10. Cited in Sabato, op. cit., p. 208.

11. In a 1973 article summarizing Supreme Court decisions for the year, the *New York Times* omitted mentioning one. "The Justices had announced that they would not revive a paternity suit in which the defendant was *Times* publisher Arthur Ochs Sulzberger"; see Bates, op. cit., pp. 54–55.

12. Anthony Lewis, cited in Sabato, op. cit., p. 212.

Part Three: How We Speak to Others
CHAPTER 6: CONTROLLING RAGE AND ANGER

1. For this insight into the nature of Moses' sin, I am indebted to my friend, Bible scholar Professor Jacob Milgrom.

2. Michael Caine, *Acting in Film* (New York: Applause Theater Book Publishers, 1990), pp. 115–117. Caine, whose book reveals him to be a person of considerable ethical sensitivity, offers a useful and reliable guideline for anyone whose bad temper can cause him or her to say unfair things: "Never, ever, under any circumstance, shout at anybody who is lower on the ladder than you are." In other words, don't scream at anybody who doesn't have the right to shout back. As Caine explains, to do so is to take "a monstrously unfair advantage" (p. 117).

3. Gelles convincingly speculates that some people get drunk "knowing their inebriation will give them an excuse for violence." He probably doesn't mean physical violence alone. In Edward Albee's brilliant play *Who's Afraid of Virginia Woolf?* a couple get drunk, in large measure, it would appear, to enable them to say the most vicious things to each other, all the while knowing that they have a readily available excuse the next morning, something along the lines of "I'm really sorry. But don't hold me responsible for things I say when I'm drunk."

Whether one spouse will hold the other responsible eventually becomes an irrelevant issue, since the abuse will have wreaked its damage. For just as each would not have fallen in love had his or her partner acted with such rage during their courtship, so too their love won't endure if the spouse refuses to curb his or her anger.

4. I am indebted to Rabbi Zelig Pliskin for this commonsensical proof that we have far more power to control our anger than many of us are willing to admit.

5. Moses Maimonides, *Mishneh Torah,* "The Laws of Personality Development," 1:4.

6. Ibid.

7. Aristotle, *The Nicomachean Ethics*, "The Virtue Concerned with Anger," 4:5.

8. Carol Tavris, *Anger* (New York: Touchstone, 1989), p. 152.

CHAPTER 7: FIGHTING FAIR

1. Babylonian Talmud, *Bava Mezia* 84a.

2. The story also contains a great puzzle. Although Rabbi Yochanan was Resh Lakish's teacher and the greater sage, it was his behavior, not Resh Lakish's, that seems more worthy of censure. After all, it was he who, by mocking Resh Lakish's background as a gladiator and a thief, introduced a personal attack into an intellectual argument. To do so was not only cruel (Jewish law considers it a serious sin to remind a penitent of his earlier misdeeds [Babylonian Talmud, *Bava Mezia* 58b]), but also in no way advanced the position Rabbi Yochanan was supporting.

Thus, Resh Lakish's pained, sarcastic response has always struck me as understandable, even reasonable. Yet the Talmud seems to suggest that because Resh Lakish's comment hurt Rabbi Yochanan's feelings, he was afflicted with a mortal illness.

His sickness and death seem so unjust that I am moved to suggest a more "naturalistic" explanation for them. Resh Lakish had become religious solely because of Rabbi Yochanan's influence. Thus, when his teacher humiliated him in public, Resh Lakish became so despondent, he lost the will to live. We know that great emotional stress suppresses the immune system and leaves the body extremely vulnerable to serious illness. Resh Lakish's illness paralleled Rabbi Yochanan's subsequent collapse; in both cases, extreme mental depression led to a sharp physical decline, and death.

CHAPTER 8: HOW TO CRITICIZE, AND HOW TO ACCEPT REBUKE

1. Isaac Asimov, *I, Asimov: A Memoir* (New York: Doubleday, 1994), p. 49.

2. Ibid., p. 51.

3. Ibid., p. 52.

4. Ibid., p. 50.

5. *Genesis Rabbah* 54:3.

6. The tone of a caring critic is precisely what was lacking in N.'s encounters with Asimov; the teacher's undisguised hostility hurt the young writer as much as his words.

7. Moses Maimonides, *Hilkhot De'ot*, "The Laws of Personality Development," 6:7.

8. It's hard to know what motivated N. In the first instance, perhaps he believed that dismissing Asimov's writing with a four-letter word would ingratiate him with his other students. But when he offered his private criticism, his motive was probably sadistic. He clearly resented having to include in the school's journal a story he didn't like. Because he derived no pleasure out of publishing the story, he wanted to ensure that Asimov had none either. Whatever justification there could be for N.'s initial behavior (although the criticism was crudely offered, it was intended to help Asimov develop his writing skills), there is none for the second gratuitously cruel and maliciously dismissive attack.

9. For example, the teacher could have selected several sentences that did not work and have demonstrated how this actually weakened Asimov's writing.

10. Cited in Zelig Pliskin, *Love Your Neighbor* (Jerusalem: Aish HaTorah Publications, 1997), pp. 287–288.

11. Babylonian Talmud, *Yevamot* 65b.

12. Rabbi Shlomo Yosef Zevin, *A Treasury of Chassidic Tales on the Torah* (Jerusalem and New York: Mesorah Publications, Ltd., in conjunction with Hillel Press, 1980), pp. 189–191; I have based this excerpt on Uri Kaploun's translation of Rabbi Zevin's rendering of the tale.

13. Babylonian Talmud, *Arakhin* 16b.

14. Dov Katz, *T'nuat Ha-Mussar* (The Mussar Movement), 5 vols. (Tel Aviv: 1945–1952), vol. 1, pp. 315–316.

CHAPTER 9: BETWEEN PARENTS AND CHILDREN

1. Babylonian Talmud, *Ta'anit* 20a–b.

2. Miriam Adahan, *Raising Children to Care: A Jewish Guide to Childrearing* (Spring Valley, N.Y.: Feldheim, 1988), p. 161.

3. Cited in Doris Kearns Goodwin, *No Ordinary Time: Franklin and Eleanor Roosevelt: The Home Front in World War II* (New York: Simon and Schuster, 1994), p. 93. The effect of Eleanor's mother's disapproving, unloving attitude was so profound that when her mother died a month after Eleanor's eighth birthday, "Death meant nothing to me, and one fact wiped out everything else—my father [who had been away for a long time would be] back, and I would see him very soon" (p. 94).

4. Babylonian Talmud, *Shabbat* 10b.

5. Lewis Grizzard, *My Daddy Was a Pistol, and I'm a Son of a Gun* (New York: Dell, paperback, 1986), p. 11.

6. Babylonian Talmud, *Tamid* 32a.

CHAPTER 10: THE COST OF PUBLIC HUMILIATION

1. Babylonian Talmud, *Bava Mezia* 58b.

2. The incident concerning the $500,000 donation is recounted in Stephen Bates's *If No News, Send Rumors: Anecdotes of American Journalism* (New York: Henry Holt, 1981), p. 142. I very much hope that in citing this anecdote and others, I have not further embarrassed the individuals involved, and

apologize if I have done so. However, it is very difficult, if not impossible, to make people aware of how terrible shaming another person in public is without citing specific instances in which this has happened. I have tried to cite only cases that already have been widely publicized or where I could conceal the participants' identities.

This is one of two instances I know in which the *St. Louis Post-Dispatch* seems to have gone out of its way to humiliate people. In *Scandal: The Culture of Mistrust in American Politics* (New York: Times Books, 1991), Suzanne Garment reports the case of John C. Shepherd who in April 1988 was offered the post of deputy attorney general in the Reagan administration. Shepherd was a widely respected St. Louis attorney, and a past president of the American Bar Association.

The day after he was nominated, the *Post-Dispatch* published a story about him that contained the charge by Denise Sinner, an ex-bookkeeper in Shepherd's law firm, that he had had an affair with her. In fact, Sinner had embezzled $147,000 from the firm, and at her recently concluded trial had claimed that Shepherd had allowed her to steal the money because of their relationship.

The jury had rejected Sinner's rather implausible defense, and convicted her. The *Post-Dispatch* reported that Sinner, who had not yet been sentenced, now desired to testify at Shepherd's confirmation hearings. Within days, her charges, which were totally without foundation, were being headlined in other parts of the country (for example, on page one of the New York *Daily News*). Two weeks later, the newspaper noted that its reporters had investigated Sinner intensively and found that nearly every significant detail she provided about her background had been proven false. From the perspective of ethics, as opposed to the *Post-Dispatch*'s journalistic practice, this investigation should have been conducted *before* the article containing Sinner's defamation of Shepherd appeared. By the time the newspaper's "correction" was made, Shepherd had withdrawn as a nominee, citing the intolerable pressures on himself and his family.

Ten days later, the judge who sentenced Sinner called her a "pathological liar" (pp. 289–290).

3. Babylonian Talmud, *Bava Mezia* 58b.

4. Atwater's response that he wouldn't answer charges made by a person "hooked up to jumper cables" is cited in *Feeding Frenzy: How Attack Journalism Has Transformed American Politics* (New York: Free Press, 1991), p. 161;

his apology to Turnipseed is noted on p. 271, note 65. Unfortunately, the evil generated when one person publicly humiliates another often grows with time. In 1988, Turnipseed, still nurturing a grudge against Atwater, helped spread a vicious, and untrue (although Turnipseed apparently thought it was), rumor of adultery against Republican vice-presidential candidate Dan Quayle. Turnipseed's grievance was almost certainly not against Quayle, but against his campaign manager, Lee Atwater.

5. Seymour Wishman's abusive cross-examination of the complainant in the rape case, and his subsequent pangs of guilt, are discussed in his *Confessions of a Criminal Lawyer* (New York: Viking Penguin, 1982), pp. 3–18. According to Wishman, the justification criminal lawyers often offer for their brutal behavior, "I was only doing my job," has increasingly come to sound like a Nazi affirmation (p. 151).

6. George Bernard Shaw, *Saint Joan* (New York: Viking Penguin, 1951), p. 154.

7. The story about President Truman and the university student is told in Merle Miller, *Plain Speaking: An Oral Biography of Harry S. Truman* (New York: Berkley Publishing, distributed by G. P. Putnam, 1974), pp. 401–402.

8. James Hume, *The Wit and Wisdom of Winston Churchill* (New York, HarperCollins, 1994); pp. 197–198. I have added the words "will then be," since the story is a bit unclear without them.

9. Merle Miller, op. cit., pp. 401–402.

10. Cited in Rabbenu Bachya, *Encyclopedia of Torah Thoughts,* translated and annotated by Rabbi Dr. Charles B. Chavel (New York: Shilo Press, 1980), p. 210. Rabbenu Bachya attributes this teaching to a book called *Ma'asei Torah,* written by the third-century rabbi Judah the Prince; recent scholarly investigations suggest, however, that this work was composed several hundred years later.

11. Babylonian Talmud, *Bava Mezia* 59b.

Notes

CHAPTER 11: IS LYING ALWAYS WRONG?

1. Babylonian Talmud, *Ketubot* 16b–17a.

2. "On Lying," in *Treatises on Various Subjects,* R. J. Deferrari, ed. (New York: Catholic University of American Press, 1952), vol. 14. Responding to Augustine's prohibition, Catholic tradition introduced the concept of the "mental reservation." An example: If a feverish patient asks a doctor what his or her temperature is, the physician is permitted to answer, "Your temperature is normal today," while making the "mental reservation" that it's normal for someone in the patient's precise physical condition (Charles McFadden, *Medical Ethics,* cited in Sissela Bok, *Lying: Moral Choice in Public and Private Life* [New York: Vintage Books, 1989]).

3. Cited in Michael Berenbaum, *The World Must Know* (Boston: Little, Brown, 1993), p. 169.

4. "On a Supposed Right to Lie from Benevolent Motives," in *The Critique of Practical Reason,* Lewis White Beck, ed. and trans. (Chicago: University of Chicago Press, 1994), pp. 346–350.

5. Bok, op. cit., p. 44. The kind of potentially murderous commitment to truth espoused by Kant prompted Thomas Jefferson to note in a letter to a friend: "State a moral case to a ploughman and a professor. The former will decide it as well, and often better than the latter, because he has not been led astray by artificial rules." (cited in David Nyberg, *The Varnished Truth: Truth Telling and Deceiving in Ordinary Life* [Chicago: University of Chicago Press, 1992], pp. 205–206).

6. Babylonian Talmud, *Yevamot* 63a, based on Jeremiah 9:4.

7. Babylonian Talmud, *Sukkah* 46b.

8. Babylonian Talmud, *Hullin* 94a.

9. Ibid.

10. Babylonian Talmud, *Yevamot* 65b.

11. *The Fathers According to Rabbi Nathan,* 12:3.

12. See Zelig Pliskin's discussion of this point in *Love Your Neighbor* (Jerusalem: Aish HaTorah Publications, 1977), pp. 206–207. The ruling permitting

lying in such a case is found in the Haffetz Hayyim's "Laws of *Rechilut* [talebearing]," 1:8.

13. Somerset Maugham, *A Writer's Notebook* (New York: Penguin Books, 1993), p. 286.

14. Graham Greene, *The Heart of the Matter* (New York: Viking, 1948), p. 59.

15. Norman Cohn, *Warrant for Genocide* (New York: Harper and Row, 1966, 1967).

16. Despite his mid-twentieth-century reputation as one of the world's greatest historians, Toynbee seems to have possessed a strangely limited commitment to telling the truth. In his later years, he compared Zionism to Nazism, going so far as to argue that "on the Day of Judgment, the gravest crime standing to the German Nationalists' account might be, not that they had exterminated a majority of Western Jews, but that they had caused the surviving remnant of Jewry to stumble [and perform Nazi-like acts against the Arabs of Palestine]" (*Study of History*, vol. VIII [New York: Oxford University Press, 1947–1957], p. 290n). On another occasion, he wrote: ". . . in the Jewish Zionists I see disciples of the Nazis" (see *Reconsiderations*, pp. 627–628). Whatever one's position vis-à-vis the Arab-Israel conflict, it's a lie to argue that any symmetry exists between the Nazis' behavior toward the Jews and the Jews' toward the Palestinians. Toynbee had every right to oppose Zionism; he had no right to lie about it. As Bernard Baruch put it: "Every man has a right to his own opinion. But no man has a right to be wrong in his facts." Least of all, one might add, a historian.

17. The selection from *Mein Kampf* is printed in Philip Kerr, ed., *The Penguin Book of Lies* (New York: Viking, 1990), p. 525. Hitler contrasted the effective Allied propaganda with what he considered ineffective German propaganda. According to him, the German press depicted Allied troops as ineffective and somewhat ridiculous. When German troops confronted Allied soldiers and realized that what they had been told was untrue, they became demoralized. Elsewhere in Kerr's unusual, very useful anthology, he reprints a 1938 speech by MP Harold Nicolson, who declared: "During the War [World War I] we lied damnably." When another member called out, "Splendidly," Nicolson responded: "No, damnably, not splendidly," going on to note that a careful reading of *Mein Kampf* reveals that Hitler

gained some of his ideas about propaganda and lying from the Allied effort: "[Hitler] thought it tremendous. He admired it very much" (pp. 352–354).

Kerr also reprints part of the Bryce Report, the official 1915 British document containing allegations of German atrocities in Belgium and France. He notes that the report "was largely invented," particularly the repeated accusations that German troops, acting under orders, cut off civilians' hands, burned whole families alive, and bayoneted little children (pp. 294–297).

18. Gloria Steinem, *Revolution from Within* (Boston: Little, Brown, paperback, 1992, 1993), p. 222.

19. Naomi Wolf, *The Beauty Myth* (New York, William Morrow, 1991; Anchor Books, paperback, 1992), pp. 180–182 and 207.

20. Joan Brumberg, *Fasting Girls: The Emergence of Anorexia Nervosa as a Modern Disease* (Cambridge, Mass.: Harvard University Press, 1988), pp. 19–20; cited in Christina Hoff Sommers, *Who Stole Feminism?* (New York: Simon and Schuster, 1994), p. 11.

21. The discussion concerning the untruths spread about the anorexia nervosa fatalities is cited in Sommers's book, ibid., pp. 11–12.

Part Four: Words That Heal

CHAPTER 12: WORDS THAT HEAL

1. The Art Buchwald column is reprinted in Jack Riemer, ed., *The World of the High Holy Days* (Miami: Bernie Books, n.d.), pp. 203–204.

2. Ibid., pp. 316–321. Rabbi Riemer has, I believe, both written on and collected the most powerful material with which I am familiar on the ability of words to console and heal. In writing this chapter, I am profoundly indebted to Riemer for his pathbreaking work in this area.

3. *Ethics of the Fathers* 6:3.

4. Palestinian Talmud, *Bava Mezia* 2:11.

5. Babylonian Talmud, *Berakhot* 58a.

6. Ibid., p. 355.

7. Deborah Tannen, *You Just Don't Understand: Women and Men in Conversation* (New York: William Morrow, 1990; Ballantine Books, paperback, 1991), pp. 113–114.

8. Richard E. Lapchick, in Ralph Keyes, ed., *Sons on Fathers* (New York: Collins, 1992), pp. 32–33.

Part Five: What Do We Do Now?

CHAPTER 13: INCORPORATING THE PRINCIPLES OF ETHICAL SPEECH INTO DAILY LIFE

1. Solomon Schimmel, *The Seven Deadly Sins* (New York: Free Press, 1992), p. 83.

2. Harold Kushner, *When All You've Ever Wanted Isn't Enough* (New York: Pocket Books, 1987), p. 187.

Index

Index

Index

Hayyim, Haffetz, xxi, 46–47
health problems, 47
Heart of the Matter, The (Greene), 141–142
Hebbel, Friedrich, 181
Hellman, Lillian, 33–34, 173, 192*n*–193*n*
Hillel, Rabbi, 133–134
Hispanic Americans, 185–186
Hitchcock, Alfred, 53
Hitler, Adolf, 6, 7, 143, 180, 205*n*–206*n*
Hiyya, 137
Hiyya, Rabbi, 118–119
Holocaust, 8, 134, 135*n*, 142–144, 157–158, 180, 190*n*
homosexuality, 20–21
honoraria, 64*n*
Hoover, J. Edgar, 59, 198*n*
horeh (parent), 110
hospitality, 15–16, 138, 180
"How are you?," 156, 163
Hume, James, 127
humiliation, 118–132
   anger and, 78, 129, 132
   apologies for, 121–123, 126–128
   avoidance of, 129–132, 139–140
   of children, 94–95, 97, 109–110, 114–115
   consequences of, 118–132, 179
   criticism and, 93–95, 97
   lying and, 139–140, 179–180
   public, xix, xx, 22*n*, 35, 46–54, 114, 118–132, 178–179, 185, 201*n*–203*n*
Hymel, Gary, 127*n*
hypnosis, 124–125
hypocrisy, 61, 62*n*

Iago, 33, 173, 193*n*
Ibn Gabirol, Solomon, 14
I Confess, 53
illness, 47–48, 199*n*–200*n*
"I love you," 156, 161
immune system, 199*n*–200*n*
"I'm sorry," 156, 164

"Incident" (Cullen), 189*n*
innuendo, 9, 23
insults, 77, 108–109
Isaac, 69
Israel of Vishnitz, 99–101

Jackson, Andrew, 4
Jacob, 69, 116
Jefferson, Thomas, 204*n*
Jews:
   laws of, xix, 21–23, 43–44, 46–47, 50, 53–54, 132, 138, 140
   Orthodox, 170
   prejudice against, 6, 32*n*, 173, 190*n*
Job, 19
Johnson, Samuel, 37–38
Joseph, 116
journalism, 20–21, 25–26, 28–30, 55, 56, 61, 64–65, 119–121, 124, 171, 184, 196*n*–198*n*, 202*n*
Judah the Prince, 118–119, 132
Judges, 69

Kant, Immanuel, 134–135, 136, 179, 204*n*
Keneally, Thomas, 157–158
Kennedy, Edward M., 7, 190*n*
Kennedy, John F., 58–59, 197*n*
Kerr, Philip, 205*n*, 206*n*
Kienzle, William X., 53, 196*n*
Kimelman, Reuven, 163
King, Martin Luther, Jr., 59–60
Kings, 111
Kissinger, Henry, 39, 40
Knot, Andy, 32
Knowledge Explosion, The, 146
Koch, Ed, 24–26, 192*n*
Koppel, Ted, 39
Kronenberger, Gottfried von, 113
Kushner, Harold, 69, 182

Landers, Ann, 146
language:
   abusive, *see* abuse, verbal
   author's lectures on, xvii–xviii
   context of, 25–26

Index

Index